Maralinga
The Anangu Story

Yalata and Oak Valley Communities,
with Christobel Mattingley

ALLEN&UNWIN

Contents

Tjukurpa
The Story of the Land

Long time ago, before whitefellas came, Anangu lived on their lands for thousands and thousands of years. The land was their life. They loved the land. They cared for the country. They knew all its secrets and they taught those secrets to their children and their children's children, *tjamu* to *tjamu* (grandfather to grandson), *kapali* to *kapali* (grandmother to granddaughter).

There was a lot to learn. *Nyitayira tjuta* (boys) learned what boys had to learn. *Kungka tjuta* (girls) learned what girls had to learn. As *tjitji tjuta* (children) grew up into adults, they went on learning. Young men learned what men had to know. Young women learned what women had to know. And *tjilpi* (the old people) passed on their knowledge and wisdom to the next generations. They taught them their songs. They taught them their dances.

Anangu knew the land – its sandhills, its spinifex, its lakes and its valleys. They knew its rockholes and where to find water. They knew its trees and its bushes and where to find plants for food and medicine. They knew its rocky outcrops and where to find ochre for ceremonies.

They celebrated the land which gave them life. They knew all its creatures – its animals and birds, its reptiles and insects. They celebrated them in their *inma* (songs and stories and dances).

Anangu knew the sky, its stars and its moon. They knew its sun and its shadows. They knew its winds, from north, south, east, west. They knew the smells and the colours of the land, the pungence of eucalypts and the sweet scent of flowering mallee, the green of mulga and myall, the gold of spinifex, the grey of saltbush, and the blue of bluebush. They knew the earth, red and strong under their feet. That earth was their life.

The earth made Anangu proud and strong. It made them happy. They knew who they were. They knew where they belonged. They were free and they travelled their country from north to south, from east to west. They knew the red earth and the rocks, from the soles of their feet right up through their hearts and minds and memories. Memories that went back thousands of years, hundreds of generations through all the Anangu who had lived, and loved that precious land. Memories that went back to the Dreaming, the Ancestors and the sacred places.

Anangu were a people rich in stories, songs, tradition and knowledge. That is the *Tjukurpa*, the Dreaming, which kept their spirits strong. •

Water

Kapi (water), so precious in Australia, is basic for survival. Nobody can live without it. In the desert it is very scarce indeed. Yet for many thousands of years Aṉangu have lived in the western desert regions of southern Australia. The desert has been their *ngura*, their home. For generation after generation they cared for every water source across their country – every *wanampitjara* (spring), every *tjintjira* (claypan), every *kapi piṯi* (soak), every *tjukuḻa* (rockhole). They knew and cared for every plant whose roots could supply valuable moisture, and in early mornings they collected dew with sponges made of grass.

Aṉangu life revolved around water sources – visiting them, using them wisely, protecting them, celebrating them with ceremonies, dances, songs and stories. The desert people travelled in small family groups, because in most places there was not enough water for bigger groups.

Rain in the region is unpredictable, most falling at the end of winter or from the tail of northern tropical monsoons. Then the people could travel into areas where normally no water is found, to care for the country. After rain, water collects for a while in claypans, where children and adults loved to swim. Sometimes, with their digging sticks, Aṉangu built earthen dams on claypans, with channels to collect the water. They placed bushes on the surface to reduce evaporation.

In times of drought people would gather at one of the few permanent water resources, *Yuldi* (Ooldea Soak), in the far south-east of the country. The Soak, in a wide depression of white sand, encircled by big red sand dunes, where black oak, mulga and other shrubs, spinifex and grasses flourished, had always been very important to Aṉangu. Groups from all across the desert met there for ceremonies and trade, and each group camped in its own area according to the direction from which they came. The people dug wells by hand, and when they left they allowed the sand to fall back in, to conserve the precious water.

They also covered *tjukuḻa* (rockholes) with stone slabs to cut down water loss and to keep out animals. *Tjukuḻa* were more permanent water sources and each had a name and a story. Permanent waters were usually home to *waṉampi* (carpet snakes), revered as guardians of the site.

Alice Cox, the oldest lady at Oak Valley, remembers: 'As a child I would walk around in line with family, with my parents and grandparents, to find water in the rockholes. Walked around in spinifex country, sandhill country, through rockhole country. *Waṉampi* was everywhere in all the rock country. Aṉangu would look at rockhole and *Waṉampi* would send water out. If we found water we would go and tell other families where *kapi* was.'

When approaching a rockhole, Anangu took great care not to disturb the snake spirit. Women and children could only approach with guidance from men. Alice recalls:

'One of the ladies was nearly grabbed in the water. It was a big water snake, *Wanampi*. Old people said, "It's dangerous for kids to hang around. The snake might grab them." I was really scared. I didn't want to hang around.'

Yvonne Edwards also remembers how the old people would wake *Wanampi* to give them water:

'Some waterholes, you know, the thing the old people talk about – the water snake. They throw a stone. Wake him up. They say, "We got no water. Can you give us some water?" Snake hears. He throws water up and they fill their kangaroo-skin bags.'

3

Aru and Makuru

Three Anangu ladies, Freda Beara, Gracie Peters and Girlie Watson, told this story of the two brothers Makuru and Arunya. Like many Aboriginal stories it teaches a lesson and describes how the landscape was formed.

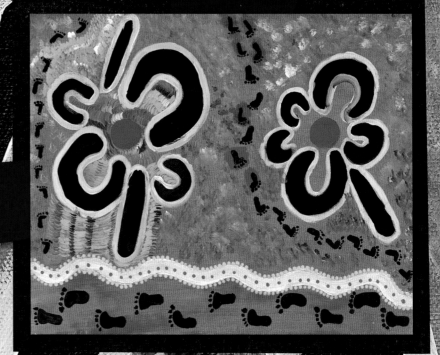

'Long time ago there were two brothers. They came from the north and had travelled all around. The older brother was Makuru. He was greedy. The younger brother was called Arunya. He was a little bit blind. Makuru always gave Aru the same dirty water to drink. It had sticks, stones and dirt in it. Arunya was always thirsty. Makuru hid his water. The younger brother had no meat or firewood either.

One day Makuru caught his younger brother sleeping with the wrong woman, so he tipped out his water. Arunya was really thirsty. He could smell the water which had come from the spinifex country up north and he thought, "That's my water." Arunya put a hole in Makuru's water bag with his stick and the water squirted everywhere.

Makuru had gone for a walk. He looked back and saw water squirting everywhere, so he ran back and saw his brother sitting down. He picked him up and put him on his shoulders so that he wouldn't drown. But they both drowned and turned into stone. The two stones are still at Eucla.

After the brothers drowned, the water ran into the sea, leaving the cliffs and a large swampy plain which looks like an old dried-up lake. A lot of women came down from the north. They were following the footprints of the two men along the creek and the smell of water on the south wind. They saw that the two men had drowned. So they put the sandhills and the cliffs along the coast to stop the water from coming in and drowning everyone.

On the way to Eucla on the coast there are two big round rockholes called Aru and Makuru.

If you look at the Milky Way at night time you will see two bright patches of stars. These remind us of the two brothers. *Tjukurpa irititja*. This is a story from long time ago.' •

Bush Tucker

Anangu were expert in finding *kuka* (food) in their harsh environment. Men, trained from their youth, were skilled hunters of *malu* (red kangaroo) and *kalaya* (emu). Sometimes they had to walk many miles and camp out to find a kangaroo. Then the hunter would carry it back to camp on his shoulders, to be cooked in its skin and shared with his family and his wife's family.

Women knew how to find smaller game, such as *watu* (wombat), *tjirilya* (echidna), goanna, lizard and snake. Alice Cox remembers her mother digging out snakes: 'Muruntu was a quiet one, easy to kill.'

Maku (witchetty grubs), found in the roots of certain shrubs, also had to be dug by women. Yvonne Edwards and Brenda Day told about hunting for *kalta* (sleepy lizard) in the book *Going for Kalta*, which won a Children's Book Council of Australia Book of the Year Award in 1998. Yvonne Edwards tells now about hunting for wombat at Monburu (Ooldea Tank): 'Three or four ladies would go with their dogs for *watu*. "Here's a nice hole." They had a little tool. Wire. Just dig, dig, dig. Hole getting deeper. She'd tell the other lady, "Dig over there. That's where he might come out." They'd have no dinner. They'd make a fire and sleep overnight. No blankets. Cover the hole over so the wombat couldn't get out. Hard ground. DEEP hole. You could see a woman sitting down in there.

Next day dig, dig, dig. Put a long stick in. Can sometimes see hair on end of stick and they say, "He's there!" Push the crowbar in, pull him out. Cut wombat up, put him on their head, climb over dog fence, night time. Wombats go mangy in winter eating fresh grass. Don't eat them in winter. No water, dry grass and they go fat in summer.'

Firewood had to be gathered for cooking. It took about four hours to cook a wombat, less for a kangaroo. Echidnas had to be skinned first. So did emus, and their skin saved for the feathers to be used in ceremonial decorations. Sleepy lizards needed half an hour to soften their scales. *Kipara* (bustard, known as turkey) were plucked before cooking, while eggs of the *nganamara* (mallee fowl) were cooked in their shells in the ashes.

Women and children were adept foragers and gatherers of fruits, berries and seeds, often walking long distances in their search. *Wayanu tjuta* (quandongs) were eaten in spring when they were red. Alice Cox remembers:

7

'One summer day when I was in my eighth or seventh year, I walked with my parents and other kids to look for berries. Some kids spotted *i<u>l</u>i* (wild fig), by rocks on a hill. I gathered them to taste. *Palya!* (Good!) I took them back to camp in a *wira* (wooden scoop) and shared them with other families. I told them where to find them. "Not far from camp, ten miles or five miles."'

Other sources of sweetness were gum blossoms, which were chewed, and *ngapari* (lerps), the white protective casing of some little insects on gum leaves. A special grass, *wangu<u>n</u>u*, bore seeds prized for making a brown flour for damper. But gathering the seeds, winnowing them with a *pita* (shallow wooden dish) and grinding them on a *tjiwa* (flat stone) took many hours.

Yvonne Edwards says: 'When we're travelling, in bush or just sitting down long way from shop, we share. Even when we have very little we share tucker with people who have nothing. Share water too. So next day none of us have anything.' •

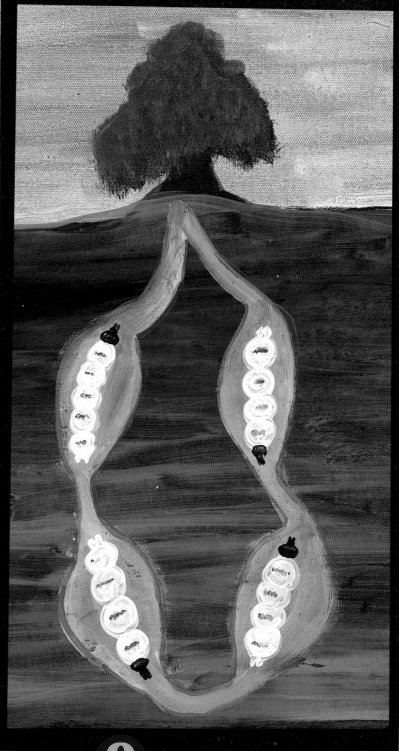

9

10

Invasion

Then, without warning, traditional Anangu life – grounded in the Dreaming, measured by the cycle of the seasons – was disrupted forever.

Although the Anangu did not know it, 34 summers earlier *walypala* (whitefellas) had arrived far to the east and settled on the land. They claimed land to which they had no connection. They called it 'South Australia'. They cut down trees and built houses, roads and fences. They brought in new diseases; different animals; different technology, including guns; different ways of making fire; and a different way of measuring time, with clocks and calendars. They took over the water supplies. Like a trail of termites, the *walypala* and their ways began to undermine Aboriginal lifestyle and culture.

Walypala 'explorers' came west and entered Anangu country. They gave their own names to many sacred and deeply spiritual places, long cared for by Anangu. And Anangu showed these strangers, who did not know the desert, where to find water to survive.

The first encounter with whitefellas is still remembered in a story about 'old Mr Eyre' told by senior Anangu men to journalist Max Fatchen in the 1960s.

In 1840, Edward John Eyre, travelling by horse along the coast from east to west, was helped to find water and grass. Eyre wrote in his journal:

I had never found the natives attempt to hide from us any waters that they knew of, on the contrary, they had always been eager and ready to point them out, frequently accompanying us for miles, through the heat and amongst scrub, to shew [sic] us where they were. I had, therefore, no reason to doubt the accuracy of their statements when they informed me there was none inland and that it took them five days, from where we were, to travel to that at the head of the Bight.

No other, they said, existed in any direction near us, except a small hole to the north-west, among some sand hills, about two miles off; these they pointed out, and offered to … shew me the place…. I accepted, and proceeded to the sand-drifts, accompanied by one of them. On our arrival he shewed me the remains of a large deep hole that had been dug in one of the sandy flats; but in which the water was now inaccessible, from the great quantity of sand that had drifted in and choked it up. By forcing a spear down to a considerable length, the native brought it out moist, and shewed it to me to prove that he had not been deceiving me.

Following the general direction the native pathway had taken, we ascended the sand-drifts, and finding the recent tracks of natives, we followed them from one sand-hill to another, until we suddenly came upon four persons encamped by a hole dug for water in the sand. We had so completely taken them by surprise, that they were a great deal alarmed, and seizing their spears, assumed an offensive attitude. Finding that we did not wish to injure them, they became friendly … and offered us some fruit, of which they had a few quarts on a piece of bark.

Having unsaddled the horses, we set to work to dig holes to water them; the sand, however, was very loose, and hindered us greatly. The natives … observed the difficulty under which we were labouring, and one … who appeared to be the most influential … said something to two … upon which they got up and came towards us, making signs to us to get out of the hole, and let them in; having done so, one … jumped in, and dug, in an incredibly short time, a deep narrow hole with his hands; then sitting so as to prevent the sand running in, he ladled the water out with a pint pot, emptying it into our bucket … held by the other native. As our horses drank a great deal, and the position of the man in the hole was … very cramped … the two natives kept changing places … until we had got all the water we required.

In 1870, well-sinkers Venning and Howie were probably the first whitefellas to see Ooldea Soak. Ernest Giles, who crossed the desert in 1875, called it the Great Victoria Desert, after a whitefella queen that Anangu had never heard of, in a faraway land they did not know existed. Giles, too, was shown the Soak and used it as a base camp. He and his companion, William Tietkens, sank and timbered a well there, and recorded rockholes, claypans and 'native dams' elsewhere. Tietkens returned a few years later, and again used Ooldea as a base. He was followed by a pastoralist who put in another well with a windlass to water his sheep. Then *walypala* came with guns to shoot kangaroos and set up their base at the Soak. Anangu were angered that they skinned the kangaroos and left the meat to rot.

After them came other explorers and surveyors, who drew whitefella maps with lines and boundaries cutting across traditional areas. In 1891–2, David Lindsay, leader of the Elder Expedition, explored the north-west. Around 1900, Richard Maurice made a number of trips and recorded five 'native dams'. In 1901, Government surveyor JG Stewart passed through Ooldea looking for a route for a proposed railway to the west. Government prospector Frank George, who came in 1904, recorded ten 'native wells'. These whitefellas put their names all over Anangu country. •

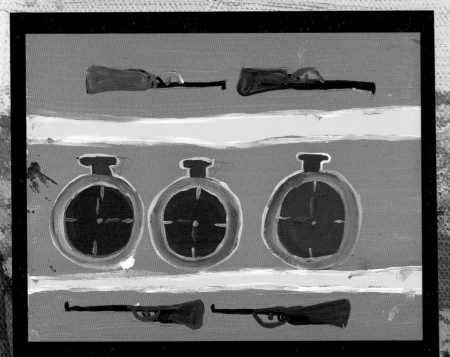

The Railway Comes

In 1912, an even more massive and sustained invasion began. Work commenced on the construction of the Transcontinental Railway from Port Augusta, in what whitefellas called South Australia, to Kalgoorlie, in what they called Western Australia.

Severe drought forced many A<u>n</u>angu groups to camp at Ooldea Soak, where water was always reliable. Here they came into contact with gangs of construction workers, who introduced them to tobacco, tea, sugar, white flour and alcohol – the 'fire drink' that 'made head no good'. A<u>n</u>angu women liked the white flour, because it was so laborious to make flour by gathering and grinding grass seed. A<u>n</u>angu men were attracted to the guns, which made hunting quicker and easier. For payment, *walypala* took advantage of A<u>n</u>angu women and soon children from *walypala* fathers were being born. Seduced by the whitefella products, the proud, independent hunters and gatherers were gradually changing their healthy, self-sufficient lifestyle.

When the railway was completed between Watson and Ooldea on 17 October 1917, its strange tracks ran across the desert like a great silver serpent. A few days later a black monster hissing plumes of steam roared and rattled into the newly built Ooldea Siding. Curious A<u>n</u>angu flocked to the line to see the apparition.

With the train arriving regularly, their isolation was finally destroyed. Then their independence was further eroded as they learned to beg for tobacco and money.

Passengers were shocked to see naked Aborigines and soon clothing was sent to make A<u>n</u>angu 'decent'. But many garments were rejects from an appeal for Europe's WWI refugees, so some *minyma tjuta* (women) were given old evening dresses discarded by Adelaide society women. They had no knowledge or means of washing and repairing clothes, so *wati tjuta* (men) and *minyma tjuta* appeared disreputable and unkempt, and soon lost their dignity, to whitefellas' eyes. They also lost what they had always known – the touch of the sun and the wind on their bare skin.

AG Bolam, who spent eight years at Ooldea Siding from 1918 as porter and station master, wrote: *See these wild blacks as they come in from the ranges, in the pink of condition, after their trip of nearly 300 miles, their skins shining with the glow of health, their carriage graceful, their movements machine-like, and then see them a month later, arrayed in the vilest of rags, themselves dirty, and their old-time customs being superseded by the traces of 'civilization', which they so readily acquire, and you see two different people.*

The trains meant that A<u>n</u>angu might travel more easily and quickly west or east for ceremonial business. But a Commonwealth Railways regulation decreed: *No native, however clean or well-dressed, may travel on the east–west line, unless special permission is given.*

Invaders have arrived at Ooldea Soak, 1920 (SLSA B452887/11)

At the Transcontinental railway line, Wynbring, 1921 (NLA)

So, many jumped the rattler, scrambling aboard freight trucks, at risk of being thrown off if discovered.

The impact of the railway was devastating in other ways too. The Commonwealth Railways acquired Ooldea Soak to provide water for the steam locomotives, and for staff at the sidings along the line. A bore was sunk and over 45 000 litres were pumped each day, steadily depleting the precious age-old resource. To improve the water, a condensing plant was built, which required huge amounts of firewood. The black oaks, which had stabilized the dunes and provided such valuable shelter, were cut down. Camel teams transported the water to the siding, and ornithologist SA White, who visited the Soak in 1917, wrote on his return a year later: *The country round has been trampled almost out of recognition.* By the early 1920s approximately 50 shallow wells had been dug at the Soak.

Then, in 1923, the water became brackish. In ten years the Soak, source of life to Anangu for many thousands of years, had been so over-exploited by whitefellas that except for one well it failed. Eight years of severe drought began, causing more Anangu to move in to the Soak •

15

Daisy Bates
and the United Aborigines' Mission

Irish-born Daisy Bates had spent many years with various Aboriginal groups in Western Australia, collecting their languages and lore, and trying to counteract the effects of whitefella activities on their lands. Affectionately named Kabbarli (Grandmother) by a group with whom she had lived east of Ooldea since 1915, she became deeply concerned at the effects of the railway on Anangu. In 1918 she set up camp between the Soak and Ooldea Siding, hoping to keep the people away from the influences that were destroying them and to care for Anangu afflicted with whitefella diseases.

Rene Sandimar remembered: 'Old Windlass was the first one to meet Mrs Bates. He sat down and made a good friend and never went back.'

Hughie Windlass, son of Jackie Windlass, was born near Kingoonya and remembered coming in to Ooldea when he was small. 'Big mob there, didn't go spinifex, sat at Ooldea. A lot of people came in, took rations and went out again for dingo scalps.' But the lure of rations was strong.

Rene Sandimar, born in her father's stony country near a big rockhole, remembered all the movements of her family when she was a child, and remembered the names of all the places and all the rockholes. 'I never saw whitefellas when I was young. But saw Aboriginal men carrying flour. They got it at Indulkana. I tasted it – *mai piranpa*, white one. Bridley, Mabel's father, had a spear for killing dogs [dingoes] for skins. They were sitting at Iltur getting [dingo] scalps to trade for rations. My sister Lucy came and met us. She told me there was a lot of flour at Ooldea. She had been there before. Mrs Bates had given Lucy rations. Came into Yooldul (Ooldea). Mrs Bates was there. She gave me a dress. I did not go back spinifex. We went in the sandhills catching dingoes [to trade] for tucker, took the skins to Ooldea. The west people came in, in Mr Green's time, women, husbands and all.'

Steven York, who married Rene Sandimar, was born north of Cook and remembered seeing his first whitefellas at Makuru. 'Jack Murray, a Pitjantjatjara bloke, had a camel. He went north from Ooldea to tell people to come in. Bates was at Ooldea when we got there. I thought she was a ghost. She used to dress up to meet the train – long skirt, high neck, gloves. There were no clothes at Makuru, but Mrs Bates dressed me up, trousers and shirt. I was still a child. We went back out again through the sandhills to Makuru, a big mob, old people, young people on foot. We told everyone about tucker at Ooldea, passing the word around. Then we came back again.'

Daisy Bates and the Duke of Gloucester at Ooldea, 1934 (SLSA B 45287/11)

The Boys' Brigade saluting the Union Jack, Ooldea, 1940s (SAMA 1083/1/4/794)

Bates encouraged the people to maintain their traditional hunting lifestyle, even though kangaroos had by now been largely displaced by rabbits introduced by whitefellas. But although Anangu still made clubs, boomerangs and spearthrowers, these weapons were now to sell as curios to tourists on the trains. She asked railway workers' wives not to sell food to Anangu, and implored passengers not to give money or tobacco. In 1920, Bates was asked to arrange an Anangu display at Cook, the next stop along the line, for the Prince of Wales. The young heir to the British throne took such interest in Anangu dance and handcraft demonstrations that the Royal train stayed for two and a half hours.

Daisy Bates lived for 16 years with the Anangu at Ooldea, but after Miss Annie Lock of the United Aborigines' Mission set up her camp nearby in 1933, and was asked to arrange a display for the next Royal visitor, the Duke of Gloucester, Kabbarli left in 1935. She wrote, *I did my utmost to arrest the contamination of 'civilization'. [But] the train was their undoing. Amongst the hundreds that 'sat down' with me at Ooldea, there was not one that ever returned to his own waters and the natural bush life.* In her will, Daisy Bates left royalties from her writing to Anangu to help them after her death.

Tommy Queama, born at Wantu, said:

'First saw whitefellas near Mimili, camel men. Heard about fat meat, sheep and good tucker at Ooldea. So went to Cook and got train to Ooldea. Miss Bates and Miss Lock there. Went back out spinifex and brought in my wife, Nellie, and her mob. I did not go back again. Everybody came in from spinifex.'

Myra Watson, younger sister of Rene Sandimar and Alice Cox, was born in 1927 between Coffin Hill and the area later named Maralinga. When she was a toddler, the family went south to Ooldea while Daisy Bates was still there. She was about eight or nine when the family travelled to Ooldea again for rations. Myra remembered that her auntie used to take off her mission clothes and hide them in a hollow tree after she left Ooldea and put them on again before she returned.

Harrie Green and his wife, Marion, arrived in 1936, and the UAM Mission was established at the Soak, '24 terrible sand dunes from the Siding', with makeshift quarters built from materials discarded by railway workers. In 1938, the government proclaimed an Aboriginal Reserve of 2000 square miles (5180 square kilometres) including the Soak. So the mission established a ration depot, a more permanent school, a church, dormitories for 60 children, a bathroom and a dining room, from recycled railway material. Men whose family received rations were expected to bring a log of wood each day to help with the upkeep of the dormitory children.

Missionary Violet Turner described Anangu as *happy, carefree people, always laughing*. But the missionaries did not try to graft Christian beliefs into their deep spiritual nature. Instead they strove to undermine and overcome traditional customs, which they saw as evil. They knew that their best opportunity to do that was through the children. So instead

Father Christmas visits Ooldea, 1930s (SAMA 1083/1/4/760)

of growing up learning Anangu ways from their parents, uncles, aunts, and grandparents, many children were taken into the dormitories and school.

Given whitefella names, because they were easier for the missionaries to pronounce, and haircuts, the children, who loved singing, were taught English, songs about Jesus, Christian values, and whitefella ways, including housework.

Anangu girls were given duties as tea girls, dish-up girls, bread girls, wash-up girls, vegetable girls, copper girls, room girls, and towel girls. Boys became room boys, wood boys and goat boys. They were given three meals a day, lollies after tea, fruit after Sunday school, and a hot bath and a change of clothes on Saturday nights. Girls received a pink hair ribbon. Boys were each given braces and a blue tie. Boys who joined the Boys' Brigade had special caps and uniforms and saluted the flag, the Union Jack.

When 126 'natives' came for their first Christmas breakfast, they were confronted by their first Father Christmas. Some were afraid. Some laughed. Adults were given cake and biscuits. Children received paper party hats.

An old cowbell called the children to meals, prayers and school, where they had to stand and sit in straight lines. At first, lessons took place sitting on the ground with the teacher drawing letters in the sand with her finger. When blackboard, chalks, books and pencils arrived from Adelaide, a brush shelter was erected, later replaced by a timber building.

Mr Minning was born north of Cook and saw two whitefellas, dingo shooters, at Makuru when he was small. He said: **'Daisy Bates was still at Ooldea when we came the first time. We went back to Makuru and back north in and out of Ooldea about four or five times. My mother and father liked the bush.'**

Missionary Harrie Green baptising Jimmy Cox, Ooldea, 1944 (SAMA 1083/1/3/569)

Now a widely respected educator, he was given the name Stanley by the missionaries. He remembers them asking his parents, who had walked from the west, if he could come into the Home. The young boy saw the trousers and braces of the Home boys and wanted braces too. But within three weeks of receiving them, he had also received a hiding from the missionaries and was often sent away 'to mind the nannygoats', the job given to 'naughty boys'.

'I ran away because they caned us. They were rough. I ran away to Coorabie and Fowlers Bay.' Later he became a baker boy, making 20 to 40 loaves of bread each day for the Home children and helpers. Finally, his natural talent was recognised and he became the teacher's assistant.

Other Home boys also remembered the discipline. Kumana Peters tried to run away, but **'they gave me a hiding'**.

School in the sand, Ooldea, 1940s (SAMA 1083/1/6/1271)

Bobbie Stewart said: ' I ran away from the Home a few times because Mr Green used to belt us if we swore.' But Hughie Windlass never tried to run away. 'Punished with no rations if we tried to run away. I grew up on the flour and sugar and got hungry for that. Because I grew up on that I stayed around.'

Children were allowed to visit the camp to see their families only on Wednesday and Sunday afternoons. Before Myra Watson started school with her sisters, she used to go hunting in her home country with her mother, who lived in camp. After she was put into the dormitory, she was allowed to go hunting only in school holidays.

When 200 Anangu came in from the spinifex, Violet Turner wrote: *Some little native girls at the Mission caught the general fever of excitement and wanted to be off to the camps. They had to be shielded from their own desires, from the machinations of their parents who were trying to entice them away.* Yet despite the missionaries' strategies, for ten years tribal influences were still strong.

Then, in 1944, sixteen young people were baptised in a well. UAM Secretary Erskine wrote: *It was no easy thing for them to take this step, renouncing the practices of their forefathers ... forsaking the superstition and darkness of heathenism to follow Jesus ... It was ration day and that meant many of the old people were in for their supplies. As they saw the group at the well they drew closer so as to see and hear better. Some of the old men seemed hard and bitter. Would it be because they thought their power was waning as many of the young men had stated that they were not going to become men in the old tribal way?* •

Baker boys Stanley Minning, Malcolm Gurney, Herbert Queama, Ooldea, 1940s (SAMA 1083/1/6/124)

Stanley Minning and Herbert Stewart, Ooldea, 1940s (SAMA 1083/1/6/1230)

Arriving at the Mission

By encouraging Anangu to stay sitting down at the Soak to receive rations, instead of pursuing their nomadic self-sufficient lifestyle, the missionaries increased Anangu dependence. Men were taught to 'work for their living' by cutting wood, pumping water, driving the horse and jinker to carry goods from the siding, scooping sand drifts away from the buildings and riding with the weekly mail to the siding. Women were taught to wash and iron clothes, to sew, to mend and even to knit and crochet.

But there was not enough work for 'all the natives'. So some young men were sent off to work on stations further east, where they were sometimes exploited and abused. On one station men were chained by the neck to trees and posts or tied up with wire, without food or water. They were set upon by dogs and shot at if they tried to escape.

In 1943 and 1944, new groups were still coming in to the Soak from the spinifex country in the north-west because of drought. Alice Cox, whose Anangu name is Mangkatina, remembers how she came to Ooldea when she was a young teenager: 'I remember sitting with my parents and other family groups, learning as I listened to them talking about *inma* (ceremonies). After my father passed away, an elder said, "We need to take Mangkatina to another place." We came travelling through the desert, walking in the spinifex country, through sandhill country, rockhole country, gathering food, playing along, having a rest, then coming to another camping place. It was where families would meet up and decide which direction they would go. Some people from Ooldea came where our *walytjapiti* (family), was camping. I was told my mother would take me back towards the south, where other families were at Ooldea.

'I was growing up, travelling with my family towards Ooldea. My family brought our *waru tjaa* (firestick) with us. It was our lifesaver, to make fire on the way. We walked through Maralinga where there was no bitumen, no soldiers. We came to a hill and spinifex bushes. We burnt them. "Why are you making smoke? *Tjunanpa*?" I asked. "So that they know we are coming," they explained.

Anangu aboard the UAM truck, Ooldea, 1940s (SAMA 1083/1/4/811)

'I was *mina ilu* (thirsty). When the people at Ooldea Mission saw the smoke they filled a bucket with *kapi* (water), took *tampa* (damper) and went and met up with our family. They were crying and happy to see us. I was *nikiti* (naked), and they gave me *mantara* (clothes), *pilangkita* (blanket), *kuka* (food). In the evening my family was led by people from the mission to the camp to be introduced to all the people. We camped beside a big lot of firewood, so we could keep ourselves warm.

'I went with my cousin and my sister's family, hunting for *rapita* (rabbits), collecting *mangata* (quandongs) and *kampurarpa* (desert raisins). It was a happy time, going out together and enjoying life around the mission, where I went to the Home. Mr Green gave me the name Alice.'

Mabel Queama, whose Anangu name is Nyarpinku, was born at Wantu (near Mt Lindsay) and brought south by her parents. 'I was a little baby girl on my mother's back and on my father's too. My mother and father walked with the family group through the desert to Ooldea. We camped near the fire with other family groups. Alice Cox was in that group. We were travelling through the desert through Maralinga before the bomb dust. Alice went ahead with people walking faster than my mother, up the sandhills, across the plains. My mother was still coming behind with me on her back, in the other group. At Ooldea my mother was met by her family in that big camp. We were introduced by the elders and stayed at Ooldea Mission for a long time.'

Alice Cox, Ooldea, 1940s (SAMA 1083/1/7/1351)

Margaret May, whose Anangu name is Kartjuku, was born in the spinifex. 'When I was a *tjitji*, five or six years old, my family walked through the desert until we reached Ooldea Mission, where I was put in school and made friends.'

Pansy Woods, whose Anangu name is Wipana, was born in the 1940s, at Forrest, near Cook on the railway line. She lived there with her family, then at Kalgoorlie and later at Cundeelee Mission in Western Australia. 'I met some of my mother's family group from Ooldea and my parents told me what to call them. I was happy to see them although they were strangers to me. I was looking forward to our next trip, asking my parents to go to Ooldea Mission. We got the train all together from Zanthus and came to Ooldea, happy to see my other family.' •

Missionary Harrie Green distributing rations,
Ooldea, 1930s (SAMA AA1/46/23)

Monday morning washing,
Ooldea, 1930s (SAMA AA1/46/22)

24

The End of Ooldea Mission

By the late 1940s, the fragile desert environment around Ooldea had been occupied permanently for over 30 years and was damaged beyond repair. The trees had been cut down for firewood, the bushes for *wiltjas* (shelters). The invading rabbits and the missionaries' goats had denuded the sandhills. So sandstorms became more frequent and the sand drifts uncontrollable. Mission buildings were riddled with termites, and water tanks had corroded. Feral cats and foxes had arrived, making game scarce. Water flow from the one remaining well was decreasing.

Problems caused by the proximity of the railway, and the lack of employment, continued to put pressures on the community. Kinship and family ties had been stressed even more because 30 single men had been sent to work on distant sheep and cattle stations, and some young couples, including Myra and Walter Watson, married by the missionaries without respect for tribal law, had been sent even further from home to Gerard, another UAM Mission on the River Murray. But the forced exodus did not relieve the pressures. There were still 300 people at Ooldea, including 50 in the Children's Home.

Hilda Moodoo's parents, Daniel and June, who had come in from the desert to Ooldea, were another of the couples sent away. Hilda, their second child, born at Barmera in the Riverland in 1952, was 18 before she met her parents' families.

Hilda remembers: 'When Father told me, "You got aunties at Yalata", I went on train to Ooldea Siding and stayed with people working on railway line. Wrote a letter to cousin at Yalata. Had to wait a couple of weeks, then truck came to pick up people from Cundeelee and Tarcoola. Rene Sandimar and Marjorie came on morning train and Rene asked, "What's your name? Where you from?" When she heard my name she put her arms around me and said, "You're my niece!" They took me and that night I camped with them.'

Daniel and June Moodoo on their wedding day, Ooldea 1940s (SAMA 1083/1/7/1475)

By 1946, another shadow was falling across Anangu land and society. Prime Minister Ben Chifley had agreed with British Prime Minister Clement Attlee to set up a joint Long Range Weapons Establishment (LRWE) to test weapons in Australia. British scientists chose an area to the north-east of the Transcontinental Railway on the Arcoona Plateau. A wealth of rock carvings and artefacts showed that it had been occupied for millennia by Anangu. But the whitefellas chose a name from a list of eastern Australian Aboriginal words. They decided to call it Woomera, meaning spear thrower. The Anangu word for spear thrower is *miru*.

Dr Charles Duguid, champion of Anangu rights, and anthropologist Dr Donald Thomson protested against the shooting of projectiles armed with explosive and possibly nuclear warheads across the Central Aboriginal Reserve. They were ignored. In 1947, the Weapons Research Establishment (WRE) built a base at Woomera with two airstrips, roads, railway and water pipes. By the end of the year the first rocket testing trials were underway.

Late in 1947, the WRE appointed Native Patrol Officer Walter B MacDougall to be responsible for the welfare of all Aborigines who might be affected by the Range's activities. Most whitefellas dismissed Anangu lifestyle as aimless 'walkabout'. But MacDougall had worked for some years at the Ernabella Mission for Anangu, founded by Dr Duguid and the Presbyterian Church. He understood that 'walkabout' actually involved purposefully traversing vast distances across the desert,

Anangu leaving to take part in the filming of *Bitter Springs* in the Flinders Ranges, 1949 (SAMA 1083/1/42/8224)

L–R <u>Back row</u>: Wowa (3), Louie (4) Injabodee (5), Betsy Bangal (6), Dorothy Nyinga (7). <u>Middle row</u>: Pansy (2), Ruby (5), Ownbee (6). <u>Front row</u>: Ninmunga (3), Ooldea, 1952 (SAMA 1083/1/3/640)

L–R <u>Back row</u>: Weewidga (2), Ronnie (3), Paddy (4). <u>Middle row</u>: Mervyn (2), Booga (3), Noonoo (position uncertain). <u>Front row</u>: David Edwards (3), Boongie (4), Ooldea, 1950s (SAMA 1083/1/3/642)

not only in search of water and food, but also to carry out rituals. At the heart of Anangu culture, these rituals were essential for the wellbeing of the land and its people.

MacDougall had an impossible task. He was expected to patrol over 100 000 square kilometres trying to establish contact with remote Anangu groups. For five years he was given no vehicle of his own and worked under great difficulties. But although he had also been appointed Protector of Aborigines by the South Australian Aborigines Protection Board, and felt genuine concern for their safety, he was expected to see himself foremost as a government employee, serving official policy rather than Anangu interests.

In 1949, 130 men, women and children were taken east by train to the Flinders Ranges to act in the British film *Bitter Springs*. The frontier story portrays a settler family and their sheep taking over a water source which Aborigines had used from time immemorial. A trooper arrives to deal with hostilities. The settlers and their sheep remain in possession, and the Aborigines end up working for them. It was another version of the bitter Anangu experience.

In 1951, the South Australian Government acquired a station property, to the south near Fowlers Bay. Whitefella farmers, who objected strenuously to Aboriginal occupation, received the more productive eastern area around Colona. The western remainder, Yalata, was retained as a longterm solution to Ooldea's problems. The people were not relocated immediately, but secret plans were being made: the Australian Government had now given the British Government permission to test atomic weapons in northern South Australia. These tests would affect a wide area of Anangu traditional country. Len Beadell, LRWE surveyor, was already looking for a test site west of Woomera.

Then, in 1952, a long-running row in the United Aborigines' Mission between its federal council and the South Australian branch, brought a dramatic and turbulent end to Ooldea Mission. On 24 June 1952, the Mission was closed.

Expelled!

Anangu were devastated. They had become used to the UAM missionaries and the support they provided. And they never forgot the sadness and confusion of the day they were told they had to leave their home.

Last day at Ooldea Mission, 24 June 1952
(Mrs M Green per Maggie Brady)

Thirty-three years later, Hughie Windlass told the Royal Commission into British Nuclear Tests in Australia about the trauma: ' … before the mission was closed – five o'clock, had a meeting there that thing going to be closed – mission going to be closed. "Where you going to go?" "I don't know." "You want to go back to your home." People do not know. They was all really sad that day… Next day we went over to the mission, about 9 o'clock, – came over the radio that mission was closed – closed – and it was a real sad day. People was crying that day.'

Alice Cox remembers the turmoil, anxiety and bewilderment: 'A whitefella came to the camp and did not tell us what was going to happen. The whitefella opened doors of the dormitories, the store. That whitefella came and was arguing with the missionaries. This white man came and growled at them. People didn't know what they were arguing about.'

After the argument the people were told that the Mission was closed. They were told they must leave. 'People were lining up for blankets and rations, grabbing them from missionaries. They knew this place was closing down. Everybody all crying, banging their heads, feeling mad and lost. We didn't want to leave this place. "This is our home. Where will we go?" Everyone all crying. This whitefella told us "Big truck coming from south to take you away." He told us we had to go to Ooldea Tank on Yalata. I said, "I don't want to go anywhere. Where you taking me is not my home. We were welcomed to this place by Daisy Bates, Harrie Green." I was really upset because my sister and first cousins were going different ways.'

Pansy Woods had only been in the Children's Home two days when it was closed. 'I was crying because people didn't know where they were supposed to go.' Some went east to Tarcoola, on foot or by train. Other families went north to Coober Pedy. Some caught the train west to Cundeelee. But the government had asked the Lutheran Mission at Koonibba, which had been established in 1899, to take charge of the Ooldea people and resettle them south at Yalata. Women and children were sent by truck and camel wagon, while men walked.

The Aborigines Protection Board wanted to move Ooldea dormitory children to the Koonibba Children's

29

Home 'in order to prevent them falling into the hands of the camp natives'. So Pastor Eckermann, with two helpers from Koonibba and a policeman, went to Ooldea to arrange the transfer on that traumatic day.

Pastor Eckermann described the exodus: *the long single-file columns streaming down from the sandhills out to the plain … tall erect greybeards balancing ration-bags with loads of up to sixty pounds of flour on their heads, leaving hands free for bristling nests of spears, with wives, children and the inevitable dogs strung at their heels…*

Pastor Kriewaldt was impressed: *In spite of ragged clothes, there was a certain dignity about them. They were an extremely likeable people.*

Margaret May remembers: 'A really sad day. Four elders each called which family group he would take and which way they would go. My family went to Tarcoola by train and stayed at Bulgunnia with windmill people. We saw a truck with Hans Gaden from Koonibba Mission, and he told us, "You need to come back with me to Yalata where your family is." So we went with him and he left us at Ooldea Tank.'

Ooldea Tank, an old government tank at Monburu on the Yalata property, had a windmill and a huge sloping roof to run rainwater into storage below, which could hold one million gallons (over four million litres).

Koonibba station manager Hans Gaden also assisted with relocating the Ooldea people: *It took several months to get them all out, about 60 at a time, on trucks. For the next two years we took rations up and shifted them from tank to tank for water.*

Patrol Officer Walter MacDougall supported closure of Ooldea Mission, but he had not been advised of the date it

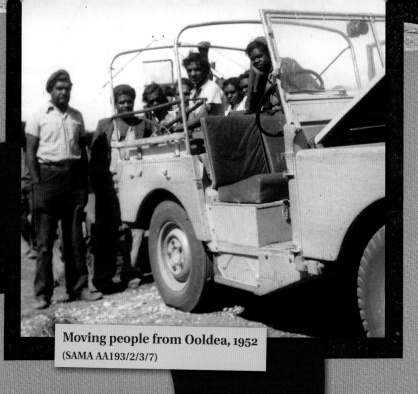

Moving people from Ooldea, 1952
(SAMA AA193/2/3/7)

was to shut down. He happened to arrive as preparations commenced and found himself involved in the task of relocating the people. He recommended that the Reserve be made a prohibited area, for Anangu safety.

Alice Cox remembers the confusion: 'When Ooldea Mission closed, Mabel and I and our parents walked to Ti Tree Station. Other people were taken by trucks and left at Ooldea Tank. But missionaries from the Lutheran Mission at Koonibba further east decided to take them to Koonibba and put the children in the Home so that they could go to school. But not Mabel. Her father would not let her go.'

Only a few children went to the Koonibba Home. Most families took their children with them, dispersing far and wide. Alice's family was moved several times. 'After a couple of weeks at Ti Tree a whitefella came with a Land Rover and took us to Ooldea Tank, where other families already had been taken. But we went back to Tarcoola, and caught the train to Ooldea Siding. We wanted to go home. But two trucks were waiting there to take us back to Ooldea Tank. We stayed at Ooldea Tank then with other families.'

Steven York remembered: 'Was there when Ooldea finished up. South mob. West mob. I wanted to go north. We were stealing the train to Tarcoola. Manager at Bulgunnia said we could stay, plenty of kangaroo there, he would give us work. But policeman came. Took us back.'

Stanley Minning and Herbert Queama walked from Ooldea to Tarcoola, hoping to go north and find their families. But MacDougall turned them back. So they jumped the rattler and returned to Ooldea Siding. Mr Minning remembers vividly: 'No mother. No uncles. No brothers. No one. Gone. All gone.' They had been sent west. With a buggy and camels he went west in search of them. But did not find them. So he also ended up at Yalata.

There the once free-ranging Anangu were made even more dependent. Sitting down. On land that was not their own. Waiting. Waiting for whitefella water from a corrugated iron roof. Waiting for whitefella rations, which were distributed on Sunday after the church service. Waiting for the tobacco and sweets the missionaries brought when they visited. •

Yalata

At Yalata, on traditional land of the coastal peoples, 140 kilometres south of Ooldea on the edge of the Nullarbor Plain, Anangu were controlled to prevent them moving back into their country – now the weapons testing area. When the people tried to go north or west on ceremonial business they were refused rations. Ration depots were closed in places where Anangu would traditionally meet for rituals to maintain country. Groups who had already walked for hundreds of kilometres were picked up and brought back to Yalata. Permission to travel by train was restricted. MacDougall also used fear of *mamu tjuta* (evil spirits) and *putjina* (poison) from the bombs to deter people from returning to their lands.

To manage Anangu movements on Yalata, MacDougall and the Lutheran missionaries devised a scheme of Big Camp and Little Camp, supplied with water and rations by the missionaries. Families lived in Big Camp. Frail, unwell, older people and mothers with new babies were under closer supervision in Little Camp. Camps moved frequently, as was the custom. Mima Smart, now chairperson of Yalata Community Council, remembers:

'When it got too dusty, camp would move. That tanker travelled every day to Big Camp. Shop, too, and medical van. They travelled wherever the camp shifted.'

Yvonne Edwards, born at Ooldea in 1950, was moved to Ooldea Tank. She remembers: 'When camp moved, we'd walk miles. We'd camp on the way, just a fire to keep us warm, no blanket. Get up early morning. Only old peoples, women with babies taken by truck.

'When people were living in wurlies they'd go down to the tank or windmill and sit all day, doing their washing in tubs. Boil big copper for hot water, use Velvet soap and rub clothes on rock. Probably learned that at Ooldea. No washing machines, no detergents those days. They'd bring their children, cook their lunch. Ration time every week. Flour, tea, sugar, dripping. Sometimes clothes, pants for men, a dress and jumper for women, and a blanket for old people.

'Our first school was walkabout school. Wherever the camp stopped for water, there was our school. Sit on ground under tree. Blackboard against tree. Sometimes canvas awning for shade. At walkabout school we had rations.'

Mr Minning remembers teaching the little ones in walkabout school, giving them milk in the morning, potatoes and onions for lunch, and food to take back to camp after school.

Margaret May went from Ooldea Tank to Middle Yard with her family. 'At Middle Yard there was a big underground tank with rainwater. People were carrying water in buckets, carrying the bucket on their head, and the bucket would stay still while they walked.'

Yvonne Edwards remembers: 'Water buckets were dripping buckets from rations. Carry bucket on your head. Your neck ache and your back ache. Make a pad, a ring, out of shirt, jumper, a ring for the top of your head to balance bucket on. And you walk. On sports day ladies would run with bucket on head.'

Alice Cox's memory of Middle Yard is not happy. 'It was a big camp, people camping everywhere. There was a big flu. Three missionaries came with medicine. Clinic was back of ute.'

Chinnalumba Well, Yalata, 1950s (SAMA 1083/2/3/2158)

Having been through such emotional and physical stress, and subsisting on such poor rations, Anangu had little resistance to the epidemic of this introduced disease. Many died. So people never camped at Middle Yard again.

A place 50 to 60 kilometres from the main road had been chosen to establish the main Yalata base. But then, for convenience, construction began near the main road. Building materials were salvaged from the UAM Ooldea site and an ex-army hut was transported from the Riverland. Two concrete slabs were laid so the children would line up in straight lines for school.

After a time with foster parents in Fowlers Bay, Yvonne Edwards went to Yalata. 'No houses there. Only a ration shed and caravan at first.' Later, army personnel from Maralinga spent weekends at Yalata. Yvonne remembers growing up seeing soldiers and Land Rovers. 'Soldiers give oranges, apples. Sometimes played sports with us. They were good men.'

Walkabout school under trees with teacher Margaret Tischler, Yalata, 1950s (SAMA 1083/2/4/8727)

33

Distribution of rations, Yalata, 1950s (SAMA 1083/2/3/2255)

Children at Nundroo with teacher
Dick Bridley (SAMA 1083/1/4/901)

Bathtime, Yalata, 1960s
(Lutheran Archives 06447)

Washing at Chinnalumba Well, Yalata,
Rene Sandimar (L), 1950s (SAMA 1083/2/3/2166)

Boys dancing, Yalata, 1950s (SAMA 1083/2/3/2265)

Dulcie Watson and child, Yalata, 1950s
(Lutheran Archives 06519)

34

The people were deeply troubled about what was happening to their own lands, and acutely unsettled by their forced removal to this alien country. Its grey powdery limestone was so different from the red earth of the desert they knew and loved. Homesick and sad, they described this new country as *pana tjilpi*, grey earth. They said it made their hair go grey, like *tjilpi*, old people. They said it made them old to live there.

The weather was different too, colder in winter, and the *wiltjas*, made of branches, gave little protection when strong south-westerlies blew in from the sea. With 7000 sheep running on the land, bush tucker was scarce and differed from the traditional desert game. Wombat was the main meat. *Malu* were not to be found in limestone country. Nor were *maku*, because the shrubs whose roots were home to witchetty grubs, did not grow in the grey earth.

Jack Baker, Mervyn Day, Tommy Queama, Kumana Queama, Joe Smart, Hughie Windlass and two others, giving evidence at the Royal Commission into the British Nuclear Tests in Australia in 1985, said: 'We felt lonely about Ooldea, we were worrying for it. We tried to get back up there. Yes, we were worrying and ... we were sad for all of the places that we were related to, and we were worried because these places had been spoiled ... We were told we could not go back there.'

Jack Baker said: 'We thought that place [Yalata] was a little bit bad and we were still wanting to come back this way [Ooldea]... it was because the country up there was the place we were related to. We were not related to that country down south and we wanted to go back. I had been a child running around the country, and we had our food around that country, and we did not belong down south, we wanted to go back to the country to which we were all related.'

35

Atom Bombs Before Anangu

In 1953, a year after the Ooldea Mission closed, it was announced in Britain and Australia that atomic weapons were to be tested in an area which was an Aboriginal Reserve. Dr Charles Duguid and Dr Donald Thomson protested. Both had worked for many years to help Aboriginal people withstand the effects of alien invasion. But their protests about the potential dangers and disruption were ignored. The Long Range Weapons Establishment issued bland but unfounded assurances that Aboriginal people would not be affected by the trials.

NOTICE
COMMONWEALTH OF AUSTRALIA
PROHIBITED AREA
THIS AREA HAS BEEN DECLARED A PROHIBITED AREA UNDER SECTION 8 OF THE DEFENCE (SPECIAL UNDERTAKINGS) ACT, 1952. A PERSON SHALL NOT BE IN, ENTER, OR FLY OVER THIS PROHIBITED AREA WITHOUT PROPER AUTHORIZATION.
PENALTY:- IMPRISONMENT FOR SEVEN YEARS.
RANGE COMMANDER   MARALINGA
DEFACEMENT OF THIS NOTICE IS PUNISHABLE BY LAW.

(SAMA 1083/1/4/729)

Prime Minister Robert Menzies requested that Ooldea's status as an Aboriginal Reserve be revoked. Politicians and scientists, whose culture and history went back only a few thousand years in another country, regarded it as desert, open space largely uninhabited. They did not understand its importance to Anangu who had cared for the land for over 40 000 years. They knew nothing of its richness in tradition and law.

Aboriginal people were not recognised under the Commonwealth Constitution of 1901. So when Native Patrol Officer MacDougall tried to explain to officials what the lands meant to the inhabitants and the effects of whitefella incursion, the Chief Scientist of the Weapons Research Establishment, WAS Butement, responded: *He [MacDougall] is apparently placing the affairs of a handful of natives above those of the British Commonwealth of Nations.*

While the dispossessed, disoriented desert people were grieving, spiritually lost in foreign country, rebuilding a few basic community structures from salvaged material twice recycled, a township for whitefellas was being constructed in their country. With the latest technology and full modern facilities, including an outdoor cinema, a swimming pool, a cricket ground, a basketball court and four tennis courts, it was the base for the contingent of British and Australian scientists and service personnel who would be involved in conducting the British Government's nuclear tests. In 1953 the site, some 100 kilometres north of Ooldea, was named Maralinga by the whitefellas. This time they took the word from an Aboriginal language of northern Australia.

37

Because Maralinga means thunder, they thought it was appropriate to describe the sound of the explosions they would make over the next ten years. The Anangu word for thunder is *tuuni*.

The Reserve was revoked in 1954, and MacDougall took some elders from Yalata back to retrieve sacred objects. At Ooldea three old men spent a day and a half looking for two totem poles. They could not find them and finally decided they had been removed, perhaps when a missionary sold some ceremonial objects to a museum two years earlier. MacDougall hoped the removal of the objects would sever their connections with the land. But it did not. Their duty of care for their country had been instilled deep. He understood so little that he even thought Anangu could establish new ceremonial sites in the new country and their old attachment would die out naturally in time. He wrote to the Range Superintendent, *Owing to the policy of the Koonibba Mission authorities, any interest will quickly die among school-age children.*

In 1955, most of the Great Victoria Desert was declared a Prohibited Area. Without warning or consultation Anangu were officially banned from their own traditional lands and nothing was explained to them.

There were still Anangu in the desert who had avoided contact with whitefellas. They doused their fires and hid when they heard planes approaching. They hid from soldiers in trucks. They knew nothing of the devastation that was happening on their lands. How could people who perhaps had never seen whitefellas read the whitefella signs saying they must not enter their own country?

In 1959, 21 months after the last test, MacDougall reported that there were still Anangu living far inside the Prohibited Zone. From the air he had seen hunting fires close to a road leading to the test site. Thirty-four Anangu located at Wanna Lakes mentioned more people closer to Maralinga to the east. Another group of 14, including 8 children, was discovered near Lake Wyola, about 120 kilometres from ground zero. •

Fallout
The Black Mist

In a memorandum to the Prime Minister in June 1952, senior scientists Professor Leslie Martin and Professor Ernest Titterton wrote, *We are able to assure you that no habitations or living beings will suffer injury to health from the effects of the atomic explosions proposed for the trials.*

In 1953, the first two bombs, codenamed Operation Totem, were exploded at Emu Field, a claypan 320 kilometres north of Maralinga. Totem's first bomb of 10 kilotons was fired at 7 AM on 15 October in weather conditions which contravened the criteria for safe firing. It had severe effects on Anangu.

At Wallatinna to the north-east, the property nearest Emu and lying in the centre of the fallout path, a black mist with a metallic smell enveloped camp sites. It was unlike anything Anangu had ever experienced. It caused stomach pains, vomiting, choking, coughing, diarrhoea, rashes, peeling skin, headaches, and sore and running eyes. Within days, old and frail members of the group had died. Over the next year, almost 20 people camping in the region also died. The number may have been considerably higher, according to Dr Trevor Cutter who worked for the Central Aboriginal Congress Alice Springs health service, but no official records were kept. The fallout over hunting grounds was far above the recommended safe level. So afterwards Anangu were eating contaminated game.

After the black mist, Yami Lester, 10-year-old son of Pingkayi and Kanytji, could not open his eyes, and for almost a week was led around at the end of a stick. His right eye became permanently blind and later he lost the sight of his left eye. He wrote in his autobiography, *Yami*: 'When I was a young boy living in the desert, the ground shook and a black mist came up from the south and covered our camp. The older people said they'd never seen anything like it before, and in the months that followed many people were sick and many died. I don't like to think about it now, but one of those people was my uncle, and he was very sick before he died. There were sores all over his body and they looked full of pus. The sun used to worry his eyes too, and he couldn't look up, so he'd wear a cloth under his hat and hang it in front of his face. Almost everyone at Wallatinna had something wrong with their eyes. And they still do. All those Wallatinna people have eye problems. I was one of those people, and later on I lost my sight and my life was changed forever.'

Yami, who had always lived at Wallatinna, was sent by train to the Royal Adelaide Hospital for tests and treatment. Unable to see and unable to speak or understand English, it was a traumatic experience. He said: 'I had never been to a European school. I did not know about European time or days of the week or years.' He was later put in the Colebrook Children's Home and sent to the Royal Institute for the Blind, where he learned English as well as how to make brooms and brushes. He wrote: 'If I had my eyes, I would probably still be a stockman. Because I haven't, I became a stirrer.'

Years later, Yami Lester and the Pitjantjatjara Council began campaigning, trying to get the Federal Government to investigate the effects of the British testing. The Council sent Yami and his wife to Britain, where he talked on radio, at public meetings and had a press conference in the House of Commons. Finally, in 1984, the Australian Government announced the Royal Commission into British Nuclear Tests in Australia.

Yami told the Royal Commission: 'I was up early and playing with an empty can … Other people were waking up … just got the billy on the fire and others still in swags. When they heard the noise they started talking … The old people were frightened. They reckon it was *mamu* … Something that could be bad spirit or evil spirit. I only remember what I saw. It was coming from the south, black – like smoke. I was thinking it might be a dust storm, but it was quiet, just moving … through the trees and above the trees and above that again.'

Kanytji, Yami's stepfather, was born at Mimili, 'a long time ago, before there were whitefellas or their bullocks or sheep or horses'. He was mustering bullocks when he heard a bang in the early morning and saw smoke cuppatea time. 'It was different from other clouds. It was from the ground and it was black. The smoke was below and the cloud was at the top. There was like a sprinkling rain, like dropping of dew. But there had been no rain. The smell was on our clothes and bodies. We felt cold and shivery. A shiver went through the heart. I was coughing – a little bit sorry. Pingkayi got sore eyes. I got sore eyes. Yami got sore eyes. Before that Yami had good eyes. Then my grandmother passed away.'

Eileen Brown, Kukika and Kanginy, who worked on the Wallatinna Station homestead, were interviewed by anthropologists Maggie Brady and Kingsley Palmer.

Elieen Brown said: 'I saw a big cloud. It was black. The cloud passed over the homestead. On the second night an old woman died and the next night my sister died. When the first person died we shifted camp a little way. When my sister died we moved again. At the next camp a lot of people died. My eyes were sore and I could not see well. My eyes have never got better. It is like looking through smoke. We looked after a little boy who had gone blind. Yami got sick too. He could barely see. He had to be kept in the shed.'

Kukika remembered: 'Smoke came from south, brought up by light wind. The sun became bad. People got sore eyes. We were weak in arms and legs, couldn't get up and dig for rabbits. Blood came from people's noses and mouths. My two grandmothers died, and my father and mother. Before the smoke we were all okay. We were without sickness. Tommy Cullinan [station manager] didn't have a name for the sickness. Didn't know what it was. I was burying people. Shifted camp again and again.'

Kanginy remembered: 'Don't remember any sickness that happened before the smoke time. The first time there was a big sickness was after the smoke. I had never seen a cloud like it before. A bit like the sort of smoke when you burn a tyre. My father was a *ngangkari*, a traditional healer, but he died because of the cloud. I was sick too.'

Judy Mayawara grew up around Wallatinna and also worked at the homestead. 'I remember people getting sick from the smoke. Vomiting green vomit. Passing green faeces. My son Kelly went blind for a while from the smoke. Got his sight back but developed a squint. Had to wear glasses. My sister died.'

Lallie Lennon, who was at Mintabie fossicking for opals with her husband, Stan, and their children at the time of the black mist, gave evidence to the Royal Commission. '**[At breakfast time] it rumbled, the ground shook, it was frightening … You could see the top of it … just going up, black smoke … we did not know what was going to happen next. We just looked, and waited and waited, thought something is going to happen next, or the ground was going to cave in … It was smoky, just like a haze … We thought we was going to die. We reckon it was poison … I cannot explain [the smell] … It is different from that [bushfire].**'

Afterwards, her son Bruce was feverish and had diarrhoea. Her daughter Jennifer had a headache. Lallie herself felt terrible, and so did her husband. It was **'like a heavy flu'**, vomiting with diarrhoea. Jennnifer started having fits, and Lallie and Bruce developed sore eyes and skin problems. Lallie said she looked as though she had rolled in a fire. **'Head to toe. I was a mess.'**

When it was reported that the Totem 1 cloud had been seen from Oodnadatta, an LRWE meeting agreed that the Meteorological Service should announce that *the observed cloud was probably a rain cloud.*

After the second round of tests on the Monte Bello Islands off Western Australia in 1956, the program was transferred from Emu to Maralinga. Reports by Maralinga personnel of sightings of Anangu were discouraged. MacDougall's August 1956 report that

42

Mushroom cloud from atomic bomb dropped at Maralinga, 19 October 1956 (Newspix)

approximately 1000 Aborigines were in the region, and numbers were increasing because of good seasons, was ignored.

Although wind conditions were again less than ideal, Operation Buffalo commenced with the detonation, on a tower, of a 15 kiloton bomb at 1700 hours on 27 September 1956. The top of the explosion cloud rose to 11 430 metres, almost 3000 metres higher than expected, which affected the range of the fallout.

By this time a Gallup Poll had revealed that 60 per cent of Australians opposed nuclear testing on Australian soil. Nevertheless, the tests went ahead. Over the next 25 days three more bombs were detonated, totalling almost 30 kilotons for the four tests. The second was exploded on the ground at Marcoo. The third was dropped from an aircraft, and the fourth also detonated on a tower.

The Final Submission to the Royal Commission on behalf of Aboriginal Organisations and Individuals said: *The Buffalo Series should have been cancelled and not have been reconsidered until adequate measures to protect Aborigines had been demonstrated to be in place.*

A year later, despite even stronger public opposition, Operation Antler began. The Antler Series of three explosions, totalling over 32 kilotons, culminated on 9 October 1957 with the biggest bomb yet, 25 kilotons fired at 1615 hours. The official safety criteria for Antler allowed double the contamination levels of the Buffalo Series.

Altogether almost 100 kilotons (100 000 tonnes) of explosive were dropped in the three series of tests between 1953 and 1957.

The most secretive series, the so-called Minor Trials, was conducted between 1953 and 1963. Approximately 700 trials released almost 100 kilograms of radioactive and toxic elements, including uranium, plutonium, beryllium, and a large number of other radioactive isotopes. These came from dispersion of the fuel used in the weapons and from the products of the fission reactions. But no meteorological records were kept that would have indicated their spread. Safety criteria were designed to ensure that the cloud of dust did not contaminate Maralinga village, airfield and firing sites. Contamination of the land was not a consideration.

After Ooldea Mission was closed, Myra and Walter Watson rejoined their people who had walked to Yalata. Myra heard that bombs were to be let off at Maralinga. 'I was worried about my country. I grieved. I was upset about what the bombs would do to the land. My sisters asked me to talk for them to help them when people were fighting to get land rights over that land. I talked to them about the things left on the ground – the radiation. They were worried but they wanted to go back on their land and show their land to their children and their grandchildren.'

Myra was an active campaigner against the nuclear waste dump proposed for Coober Pedy, where she later lived. She declared vehemently: 'The people who have done the damage should take it away. They should please clean up the place properly. My birthplace got bombed down. The bomb ruined my country, they spoiled all my country. People died north side and west side. Fell down and died. I am sad.'

Fallout
The Milpuddie Family's Story

The Final Submission to the Royal Commission stated: *It is clear that the personnel working on the minor trials never contemplated that the lands they were contaminating would be given back to the Aborigines.*

Contamination of the ground brought severe risks to naked Aṉangu, who walked barefoot, slept on the ground, and cooked on the ground using earth, sand and ashes. Breathing the dust could lead to cancer, lung and skin diseases and other health problems. The animals in their food chain were also affected.

In May 1957, after the Buffalo Series of four explosions and before the Antler Series began, the Milpuddie family were found by soldiers near the Marcoo bomb crater, close to Maralinga – an area classified as 'Dirty'. Tjanyindi (Charlie), his wife Edie and children, Henry, about eleven, and Milpadi (Rosie), about two, had been travelling south for nearly a year, following the traditional rockhole route towards Ooldea. They did not know that the Mission had closed. Only Henry spoke some English.

Mabel Queama, Edie's cousin, explained:

'There is a special track Aṉangu walk from north to south. Charlie was a wise man. He remembered the rockholes and that's why they could make the journey safely.'

But it was no longer safe to walk through their own country. Mabel said: 'They didn't know about the bomb. And they came through the bomb smoke.'

Through an interpreter Edie Milpuddie, who had been born at Tjundrun, told her traumatic experiences to the Royal Commission. 'I did not know what was happening then. I did not know that the mission was closed. We were coming this way... At a waterhole called Unguntju we heard an explosion and the earth seemed to be moving... We saw the soldiers and activity round Emu. The white fellow spoke to Henry. He had been to school in Ernabella and he started to sing *Jesus loves me* and the soldiers heard that and understood. They told Henry that the mission was closed down; there was no food there. But we still went on.

'[After Emu Junction] we were sitting camped in the bush ... We had no water, just *kapi* from the trees, knocking it out from the root ... no pannikin ... no clothes. When we lit a fire, the white fellow saw the smoke and came in the morning. [We were] surprised when we saw the soldiers in khaki ... They put us in a Land Rover and they brought us down this way [near Maralinga].'

Edie and her family had never been in a motor vehicle before and Edie vomited during the trip. Taken to the Health Physics caravan at Pom Pom for monitoring, they were made to shower, another new experience, getting soap, which they knew nothing about, in their eyes.

Edie thought, 'There's somebody else in here too.' But it was her reflection in a mirror, which she had never seen before. Charlie and Henry were given trousers. Edie was given underwear. After being photographed and deemed to be in the 'clean' range of radiation safety limits, they had to undergo the trauma of the drive to Yalata, vomiting again on the way. When his dogs were shot as a precaution against radiation, Charlie was furious and wanted to leave Yalata, but he was not allowed.

The whole traumatic experience for the Milpuddie family became known in official records as 'the Pom Pom incident'. Personnel involved were told to say nothing about it.

Edie was pregnant, but the baby was stillborn at Yalata. She and other Anangu women believe that 'the poison' caused it. The family continued to suffer anxiety and stress from their experience, with serious illnesses and premature deaths. In 1963, Allan, two, died of a brain tumour. In 1965, Annette died at six months. Another daughter, Sarah,

born prematurely weighing less than a kilogram, developed epilepsy. Edie's son Henry was diagnosed with severe advanced tuberculosis at 24. Later he developed pneumonia, bronchial asthma and oedema. One of his daughters died in infancy of a heart condition. The other had pneumonia and developed otitis media.

After the birth of their son Roger, in 1968, Edie's husband, Charlie, went off and lived alone. Rene Sandimar said: 'MacDougall was worrying for that old man. He thought his eyes were sick because he was in the smoke. He finished with wife and talked silly. He camped self and went cranky.'

Charlie was almost blind when he died of heart failure and pneumonia in 1974. Edie's daughter Rosie developed a heart condition and lost her first baby, a daughter, in 1973. Her second daughter was born with heart problems and congenital dislocation of the hips. Her son was born with a club foot.

Henry Anderson, Carlene West, Myrtle Pennington and Darlene Stevens also gave evidence at the Royal Commission about the bombs and the damage to their country and people. They had heard the explosions, felt the ground shake and seen the strange atomic clouds. Henry Anderson said that the smoke had 'killed or hurt' important sacred places. The group was found by patrol officers who told them to walk west to Cundeelee and to stay on the road. The Anangu track west led past rockholes and other water and food sources, but the road the whitefellas had constructed had no such connections. Staying on the road as they were ordered, they had no access to water or food, so Darlene's mother, father and brother perished. •

Clean-up
Mission Impossible

Bomb sites were cleared after each series, but only to make them usable for the next test. The 1960–63 series of weapon trials used both uranium and plutonium as the fuel source. JL Symonds in his official *History of the British atomic tests in Australia* says: *The explosive nature of the tests spread this material locally. Contamination was considerable.*

In 1961, six containers of plutonium fragments were placed in concrete pits at the Maralinga Airfield Cemetery, where they remained until 1978, when they were repacked and repatriated to the UK.

In 1964, after the British Government discontinued the trials, the Operation Hercules V clean-up took place. It attempted to dilute plutonium contamination by ploughing and grading it into the soil. But it was only a temporary measure, until British authorities decided whether to use Maralinga again.

In 1966, when the 10 year agreement for use of the area was about to expire, the British notified the Australian Government that it would relinquish the site. A second clean-up, Operation Brumby, was to be the final one by the British to fulfil the agreement. It used disc-harrowing and the addition of topsoil to dilute contamination.

But insufficient topsoil was used and by making windrows, contamination was concentrated and hot spots were created. Ploughing also made collection of plutonium fragments far more difficult. No record was kept of material recovered. Burial pits also were not always recorded, and solidification of materials into concrete created more problems for a future, more thorough clean-up.

But the Atomic Weapons Tests Safety Committee reported, *Maralinga and Emu remain much as they were when chosen by the Australian and British Governments for the purpose of testing nuclear weapons: namely, they are well isolated from any population centre and are of no known significance either for agricultural or mineral development. Accordingly it is unlikely that the area will become populated in the foreseeable future.*

Like all the other whitefellas involved, members of this committee had no understanding of the true significance of the land. They thought that fencing and occasional patrolling was sufficient against possibly 24 000 years of hazard from plutonium.

According to Symonds a total of 24 400 grams of plutonium was used. About 900 grams were repatriated to the UK. •

The gates to the Maralinga Village site, 2008 (Tom Stringer)

Mabel Queama at Taranaki site, 1986 (Maggie Brady)

NO ENTRY
WARNING RADIATION HAZARD
NO MATERIALS TO BE REMOVED FROM THIS AREA

Homesick!

By 1964, Yalata had a population of 350, a water problem and an unemployment problem – history was repeating itself. Some men were employed in making cement bricks and building, others in maintaining windmills and pipelines; installing tanks, fences and stockyards; driving tractors; caring for sheep and shearing; clearing scrub for an airstrip; even fighting bushfires.

But the main source of income for many men and women was making artefacts and selling them to tourists along the highway, as they had done at Ooldea to train passengers. Missionary Barry Lindner also took artefacts to sell at Maralinga test site township. Because of the success of the artefact industry, distribution of rations was stopped in 1964 and the people, who had now become accustomed to using money, bought their own supplies from the mission store.

Mabel Queama describes making artefacts:
'Woman makes her own digging stick out of mulga. Alice makes *kali tjuta* (boomerangs). Cut them out with tomahawk, rasp them with sandpaper, make them shining smooth, paint them. Use chisel to make patterns. Carve birds, lizards, snakes, music sticks, *piti*, coolamons out of quandong wood. Margaret makes very good wombats, perenti. Very big ones. Do leatherwork too, make belts. Collect seeds and make necklaces from *tjinytjulu* (gumnuts). Crochet hats and bags.'

Mabel, Margaret May and Margaret's sister Ada Hart still make artefacts. Margaret's husband, Jack May, was also a very fine carver. His work was sought by collectors across the world, and he taught many others how to carve.

Mima Smart says: 'In those days children learned from old people, learned to make their own boomerangs to raise money to go on school trips to Adelaide, Port Lincoln. Herbert Queama used to get boys sitting under a tree in the school yard to make artefacts. Those days we had to earn our money. Nowadays parents get money from Centrelink.'

She remembers Rene Sandimar spinning hair.
'When a person pass away they cut all the hair and they keep it in a bag and they keep it to spin it to make belts, head bands, or a band to put round a baby's neck to make baby strong and healthy, and so it will sleep through the night.'

Alice Cox putting gumnuts in Rene Sandimar's hair, Oak Valley, 1980
(Maggie Brady)

Mabel says: 'But people don't spin hair, weave wool any more. Granny did. Made things to put around babies' necks. Edie [Milpuddie, her cousin] made one for my son, made it out of hair spun up her thigh. Made two myself, round ones out of wool, for my granddaughters. Make bush medicine too. Put saucepan on fire with butter. Grind up leaves with rocks. Mix with butter. Rub on sore legs. Use it for headaches.'

But the people were unhappy. They were homesick for their own country. They longed for their lands. They cried for their country. They cried for the damage done to it.

Jack Baker said: 'Heard the bomb while working at Bookabie. *Pana* (earth) shaking, smoke up north, never came south. At Yalata we are still thinking about country. But they put a block on you. Like a paddock. Shut. Piling rockhole no good now. *Kapi* no good. Wiluna rockhole we cannot trust him. We cannot trust *kapi* near Maralinga.'

Tommy Queama said: 'Soldier mob was making access road from Watson. I didn't think or worry about soldiers. I was thinking about country. I wanted to go back to the country. I didn't go back because people dropping bombs. Stories of bomb and smoke frightened me. MacDougall chased us away by frightening us about the bomb. I did not hear bombs, but saw smoke.'

Rene Sandimar said: 'My husband was worried because his country was closed. MacDougall put up signs, put wood to block the place to stop men's business. We heard the bomb and saw the smoke when we were at Nundroo [near Yalata]. *Pulka!* Really big one.

MacDougall warned us about the bomb. Said, "You have to sit down. *Ngura wanti.* (Leave your country.) Smoke *panya* (Smoke, you know). MacDougall told us we could not go back because it was dangerous. But Sandimar and the old men were feeling no good. *Ulanyi.* Sandimar was crying for his country. The bomb finished it.'

Kumana Queama said: 'We were unhappy and unsettled. We never knew anything. When we saw the soldiers we didn't know anything. I was trapping rabbits. I heard the bomb, saw dust going up north, one big one. We were frightened smoke might come this way and kill us. We saw a lot of soldiers come back through Colona. We thought it was going to be a big war.'

Veronica Bridley, Gracie Peters, Mabel Queama (L–R) walking from women's camp to Yalata, 1980s (Maggie Brady)

Colin Murka at Yalata, 1960s
(Lutheran Archives 06453)

Children enacting a nativity scene, with a real baby, Yalata, 1964 (SAMA 1083/1/4/911)

Father Christmas arrives on the back of a ute, Yalata, 1959 (SAMA 1083/1/4/876)

Dorcas Williams (Lutheran archives 06454)

In 1965, with the introduction of drinking rights for Aboriginal people, some turned to alcohol to try to forget their grief. But grog only led to more unhappiness. Arguments turned into fights. Fights became violent. People were hurt.

Women and children were frightened. Old grand-mothers and grandfathers said:

'This is not our home. This is not our land. We want to go back to where we were nice and peaceful.'

The children listened to the stories the old people told. Mima Smart, born in Penong in 1956, said:

'I like hearing stories from old people. My parents used to tell where they really came from and where their real home was. Because of the bomb at Maralinga, if it wasn't for the bomb, they would have lived in the bush. When they came to Yalata, missionaries helped them, took them to Koonibba, put their children in a home. But they didn't really want to settle. They wanted to go back to their own country.'

Yvonne Edwards was six when the first bomb in the Buffalo Series was exploded. She remembers:

'Grandfather and Grandmother telling lots of stories. They had to live at Yalata. Their home was bombed. That was their home where the bomb went off. Really frightened. They thought it was *mamu*, spirits coming. Everyone was frightened, thinking about the people back in the bush. Didn't know what the bomb was. Later told it was poison. Parents and grandparents at Yalata really wanted to go home, used to talk all the time to get their land back.'

Mima Smart remembers Rene Sandimar, who fought hard to win her people's lands back. 'She was a really strong lady. A Christian lady who would tell anybody to stop making trouble. If they refused to listen to her she would tell them off and say they should not talk to an elder like that. She was a brave lady who got up and talked all the time to the big bosses like governments, prime ministers, and all the men sat and listened to her.

Her husband wanted to go back, take their children and live in the country where she roamed around. But government said, "It's too dangerous, too poisonous to go back."

'She refused to listen. She would say, "Why did you let them let that bomb go in our land? They should have let that bomb go in their own country, not in ours, and poison their own country, not our country where we would like our children to be. We want to wander from rockhole to rockhole, hunting, gathering food, finding water."'

Rene's daughter Marjorie now has to live in Adelaide, far from the country her mother knew and loved, permanently on dialysis for kidney problems.

The missionaries still worked zealously telling Anangu about Jesus. They visited people in their camps. They held services in the bush with tea chests for altar and pulpit. They baptised infants and young children, confirmed adults, and translated psalms and passages from the New Testament. Evening shows of Bible story film strips were popular, and Father Christmas arrived each year, sometimes in a truck decorated with balloons, once on horseback and once in a horse-drawn 'sleigh'.

Girls were given white dolls and taught to decorate Christmas cakes. Seesaws, swings, a slippery dip and tyres, sack races and fancy dress parties entertained the children.

Gradually more A̲nangu became Christians as the missionaries won their respect and affection, and more parents sent their children to the Home at Koonibba for schooling. Long after the Lutheran Church passed control to the newly formed Yalata Community Council in 1975, the missionaries were fondly remembered as 'good people'.

But the effects of the clash of cultures disrupting lives and ways of living continued to take their toll. The Dreaming had been buried under new ceremonies, stories and songs. A̲nangu land, source of all life, had been poisoned. A new generation was growing up, wearing shoes on the hard grey earth instead of feeling red sand soft between their toes. Wearing clothes, washing them, hanging them to dry first on whitefella wire fences, later on rotary clothes hoists. The age-old cycle of the seasons had been fractured, broken into weeks without work, weekends with Sunday services, rolling into years of despair. Money was now master. Without meaning for their lives, without hope for the future, always organised by others, prevented from returning to their lands, people were sick at heart. Sick in spirit. Many slipped into the grip of gambling and grog.

Dismayed at how alcohol continued to destroy community health and harmony, in 1995 Yvonne Edwards, Henry Beard, Sandra Bridley and Heather York wrote this letter:

Dear Licensee Commissioner,

All the people who have been living here all their lives, the sober people – we'll just move out if they get drink back here. We'll be moving out – taking all our children. We don't want the wine here. We don't want to go back. We want to go forward.

When the wine/drink here from the takeaway – people were hurt here. We lose a lot of people – accidents on the road. People come back – drink on the side of the road. Get run over. When drinking was here kids were frightened. Couldn't sleep at night. Kids too tired to go to school. Got no money for food and clothes.

People won't be working properly in the office or clinic. People will be coming there smashing windows, throwing stones also. That's true. Tjukur mulapa. That's a true story. The lady in Penong [hotel keeper] just wants to make money. She doesn't care about people getting bashed up, losing their lives.

Elders, worried about the effects of alcohol on families and the community, organised bush camps away from Yalata. They took drinkers to hunt for their food. They shared stories – talking about their proud past, thinking about their future. Some drinkers realised they were wrecking their health and wasting their lives. They gave up the grog and became useful in the community, helping others.

Elders worried too about kids getting skinny and sick from petrol sniffing.

Mima Smart said: 'Petrol sniffing and drugs were brought in by visitors from other communities. Kids wanted to try it. And got sick.'

Girlie Ingomar said: 'Their bodies reeked of petrol. They didn't go to school. They didn't eat. They had nightmares.'

Veronica Bridley and her husband, Dickie, started a sniffers' camp out bush a long way from Yalata, so the kids couldn't walk home. Jack May, Margaret May, Mabel Queama, Albert Miller, Debbie Miller, Yvonne Edwards and others took the boys hunting, the girls gathering bush tucker. They went to the beach. They danced. They listened to stories. They were happy. They had fun.

In the video *Petrola Wanti* (Petrol No Good), which they made for the community, Mabel Queama said: 'Plenty of good food for sniffers to become strong again. Fires for cooking. Made damper. Girls made soup with vegetables. Plenty of meat, breakfast, dinner, supper.'

Veronica Bridley explained: 'Kids had to learn to look after themselves. They had to learn to think about what they would do in the future.' She declared: 'Give them love. That's what they need.' Jack May announced: 'All the kids are grown up now and married.' Yvonne Edwards declared: 'Give young people a purpose, give them jobs. Then they won't want petrol.'

Some of these people and others, with support from health and substance abuse programs, still work to try to prevent the curse of petrol and alcohol blighting the lives of young and older members of the community. Men's camps, women's camps, school and Scout programs are helping adults and children to reconnect to their culture. •

Maralinga

After the personnel involved in the tests left Maralinga, salvage rights were granted in 1974 to the newly incorporated Yalata Community. The project manager asked the South Australian Health Department if radiation levels at the site were safe for humans. He was assured there was no cause for concern. But there is now no official record of this correspondence.

Buildings were dismantled, sold and relocated all over South Australia and as far away as Queensland. Some Anangu men were employed, and their families went with them and lived in the village. The only precaution taken was to show the Aboriginal workers the 'no go' fenced areas. Geiger counters and protective clothing were not provided.

Yvonne Edwards remembers: 'When we were looking after the place at Maralinga, three or four Anangu men came to stay to help pull the buildings down. When the men were at work, all the ladies used to go to the big hall and we'd jump on the big table and we'd play snooker. The hall had everything in it. BIG kitchen with everything, plates, saucepans. We took lots back to the community at Yalata. Probably all the big bosses sat in the big flash room. All the soldiers had their meals and drinks in the bar. And everything just left there – the glasses, the pictures still hanging on the wall. One shed was full of grey blankets, sheets and pillows. We took blankets back to the old people.

'Then some of us ladies walked around. We went into every house and checked it out – doors all open. It was a real ghost town, dingoes roaming around everywhere. I had a little dingo pup. But it died. One of the women, her baby died.

'We stayed in a dormitory near the hospital. They made one part into a kitchen for us and we kept all our food in the hospital. Whitefellas stayed in the hospital. The pastor came up every fortnight to have a service with us outside. The church was really lovely – organ, altar, everything. We'd go and sit down, look at the hymn books. But we never used the church. Lovely gardens and flowers growing. We'd stand there to have our photos taken.

'We went to the airstrip. It's a BIG airstrip. A really big sign: Maralinga International Airport. Drive along, "This is where the helicopters land. And this is where the big planes land." Little bushes alongside, and big buildings. A lot of rabbits because no one was there, and we chased the rabbits around Maralinga International Airport. Every afternoon we'd go down and get rabbits, or take a spotlight at night.

'All the ladies go out for *maku*, walk, get lots, plenty there. We were going every road, lots of roads there and we followed every road. But no trees anywhere. All dead. Then we driving around in evening and we could see the turkeys sitting down on hill because there's no trees. And we cooked *kipaṟa* near where the bomb went off, on the same road where dead wood was.

'We were driving round in Land Rovers, me and some other ladies. Land Rovers left there. We went to Watson to get things, fresh meat and vegies from the Tea and Sugar Train once a week. Then if we see *maḻu* or *kaḻaya*, we'd kill them and eat them, cook them in the ashes and share them with all the other workers. Aboriginal people always share.

'I think back now there's a lot of places I've been I shouldn't have. Nobody told us anything about it. Husbands working so we went back there. Mima came after, then Martha Edwards, Margaret May came later. My husband and I stayed longest. I had two children with me, Teddy not quite one, and Dwayne

about two. When the mens go out from village to pull down shed at Kittens [one of the Minor Trials sites], bitumens everywhere and sheds everywhere. Whitefellas wanted to buy sheds. I'd sit down by tree and make a fire, cook dinner for Anangu workers. Went home when they knock off. Made a big fire near heap, sit down and yarn, and listen to dingoes. At warm nights we'd sit on top of big dry swimming pool on hill, lovely and cool, fresh air, and we could see all the lights of the train and houses in Watson.

'We followed the road bitumen to the place where the bomb went off and we were all standing there looking – a BIG hole with a big fence around it and NO TREES FOR MILES, no green leaves, JUST DEAD TREES, lots of dead animals. We were walking in bare feet looking around.'

Mima Smart says: 'We wasn't told it was dangerous and that we should wear shoes.'

Yvonne Edwards says: 'When we went back we saw this BIG crack in the ground. We dug out this crack with a front end loader – and there was new washing machines still in their boxes, fridges, Land Rovers, motor bikes – just covered over.

'Mens were itchy from pulling buildings down, scratching all night. Later they came out in sores all over their chests. I seen the men working trying to cover drums over, full of poison. Whitefellas all had masks and protective clothing. Anangu men had nothing. My husband just had ordinary clothes and they made him drive the front end loader to bring drums of poison. He had to dig the holes to bury the

drums, all the dust blowing up. Driving the front end loader to cover plutonium and put cement over it. Aboriginal fella getting all the dust on top of the front end loader. That was really poison they were working on that day. One of our sons, Teddy, got very sick. He was just a baby. He was taken back to Yalata and later to Adelaide because he was still sick. But we didn't know the place was dangerous, poisoned. My husband got sick later, died of lung cancer. Now everyone at Oak Valley has breathing problems. Everyone has puffers. Anangu men worked without protective clothing.'

Margaret May and her husband Jack went to help pull down some buildings. She remembers:
'A pipe fell on his leg. A whitefella lifted him up and took him back to Yalata. Then he began coughing and we knew something was wrong. Couldn't work any more. Couldn't go back to Maralinga. They flew him to Adelaide. Had to stay in Adelaide for treatment. Got sicker and sicker until he got asthma.' •

Land Rights
Maralinga Tjarutja

In 1962, Premier Playford had promised Anangu that when weapons testing ended, their lands would be returned to them. The British scientists left in 1966. Although Aboriginal people were granted citizenship after a Commonwealth referendum in 1967, Anangu still had to wait.

In 1975, Yalata land was transferred to the newly created Aboriginal Lands Trust, and the Lutheran Church transferred its control to an all-Anangu managing body: the Yalata Community Council. But the people were anxious to regain their traditional lands, so they began pressing the government for justice.

Discussions, begun in 1981, stalled a year later because of an election.

The new Labor Government agreed to the freehold and inalienable transfer of land to the traditional owners. But the Liberal-dominated Upper House blocked legislation until it allowed access for mining interests. The Maralinga Tjarutja Land Rights Bill was finally passed in 1984. Maralinga Tjarutja means 'Maralinga down south'.

Greg Crafter, the Minister of Aboriginal Affairs at the time, said: *The legislation as it now stands represents*

Tommy Queama and Jack Baker
with the title to Maralinga Tjarutja lands,
18 December 1984 (Adelaide Advertiser)

a compromise, but those who have compromised most are the original owners. It is their patience, perseverance and willingness to compromise which deserves the major credit for this legislation passing through the Legislative Council.

When the official documents for the land grant, in English and Pitjantjatjara, were handed over by Premier Bannon at a gathering in the bush near Maralinga on 18 December 1984, the people rejoiced. But their struggle was not over. They still sought compensation for their contaminated country.

In 1991, a delegation of Anangu elders, including Hughie Windlass, Archie Barton, Barka Bryant, and Mervyn Day, flew to London with their lawyer, Andrew Collett, to put their case to the British Government. They returned again in 1992 to pursue their demands. Finally, in 1995, the British Government agreed to contribute $45 250 000 for clean-up and compensation. The compensation money is administered by a trust consisting mainly of Anangu board members, with assistance from the Maralinga Tjarutja organisation operating in the communities.

In 2008, the people are still waiting for the handover of the Maralinga village area. •

Back to the Lands
Oak Valley

The longing for their own lands was still strong with many people at Yalata. In April 1984, when legislation finally handed the Maralinga lands back to their traditional owners, new hope for return was sparked in many hearts. A few months later, about 80 excited people, looking forward to the change, moved to camp on the Maralinga road. Gradually, throughout 1985, they were joined by nearly 150 others eager to resume the cycle of ceremonies which had been so ruthlessly disrupted for over 30 years.

With a truck, some water tanks and an old Toyota, they gradually moved north and west back into their home country, where they could maintain their links with their culture. Back into their home country to settle down on the red sand, where the wind sighs and sings and roars through the desert oaks, among the mulga, myall and mallee. Back into their home country to await the miracle of a myriad wild flowers after rain, when the ground blazes scarlet with desert peas.

They camped again at last in a valley in the sandhills among groves of ancient and beautiful desert oaks, and they called their new home Oak Valley.

Over 400 kilometres from Yalata and 160 kilometres north-west of Maralinga, Oak Valley did not have water resources like Ooldea, able to support a large camp. And its ground water contained very high levels of dissolved radium and uranium, and high levels of salts and acids. A shed tank was built. But for a whole year no rain fell and water had to be carted 160 kilometres from Watson on the Transcontinental Railway Line. It was a hard year. The camp moved several times.

Stores had to be brought in. Hilda Moodoo remembers going round with pencil and paper writing down people's orders for meat, vegetables, sugar, tea, flour, tobacco. Her husband, Jeffrey Queama, drove his own car to Yalata to collect the stores and went out shooting *malu* and rabbits for the old people. Hilda remembers how the community acquired water on wheels (a tanker), a shop on wheels in which she worked, and a clinic on wheels. By the end of 1985, the community had imposed a ban on alcohol, and had a radio, a clinic and a walkabout school. Walkabout school started under a tree, later moved under a tarp, and then into two old caravans, which were too hot to use in summer, with makeshift furniture that teachers created from stuff from the dump.

By 1991, there were access roads, an air strip where the Flying Doctor comes regularly, seven shed tanks providing drinking water, bores providing poorer grade water for other purposes, a workshop, a generator and

Boys and grader, Oak Valley, 2007 (Andrew Weller)

Artefacts created by Margaret May and Ada Hart, Oak Valley, 2008 (Tom Stringer)

accommodation for teachers and health workers. Now the community has its own store and a power station. An air-conditioned school, with computers in every classroom, opened in 2003; it strives to be clean and green. Its motto is *Nintringkunitjanku.* (I am going to learn.) Houses, aged-care accommodation and community buildings have tanks and solar units. To conserve water, all toilets are long drop, except at the health clinic and visitors' quarters. A Land Care program employing local people has established trees and revegetation. Other people work in the school, store and on community projects.

Some young men have learned to operate graders and other machinery for road maintenance, and several have found work with mineral exploration teams. Plans for a desalination plant are under discussion.

The handing back of Ooldea and its surrounding land on 12 December 1991 by the South Australian Government boosted the spirits of both Oak Valley and Yalata people, and many other Anangu scattered far beyond. Now the old people sometimes return to the scene of their childhood, where billowing green pepper trees planted by the missionaries still defy the drifting sands.

Isolation has proved a blessing in some ways to the Oak Valley community, and a problem in other ways.

61

Yalata people like to visit their relations to enjoy the peace and the opportunities for hunting and bush camps, and to take part in ceremonies. But the limited water supply, especially in the severe summer heat, and the cost of bringing in stores and equipment continues to create difficulties. Oak Valley people like to return to Yalata from time to time. So sometimes not many people are left in Oak Valley.

But Mr Minning and older ladies Alice Cox, Pansy Woods, Margaret May, Ada Hart, Mabel Queama, who remember the people's story right back to the Mission days at Ooldea, work hard to pass on their knowledge and encourage Anangu crafts and heritage. Sitting around the campfire with their dogs, carving and chiselling the mulga and quandong woods they know so well, the ladies create the *ngintaka* (goanna) and *wira* for which they are renowned.

Mr Minning remembers acting in the film *Bitter Springs* in 1949, and beginning his teaching career at Ooldea. He has worked for 55 years in Anangu schools, teaching children and mentoring other Aboriginal Education Workers. In 1971, he and two AEWs from other communities were chosen to study in Adelaide, where he gained teaching qualifications. He has visited other Anangu schools at Ernabella, Indulkana, Fregon and Amata as well as teaching for many years at Yalata and finally at Oak Valley. He has contributed much to the Oak Valley community through his example and knowledge, and has inspired and mentored generations of young Anangu people.

Mr Stanley Minning, Ooldea Soak, 2008 (Tom Stringer)

Music plays an important part in strengthening the spirit of the community at Oak Valley. The railway, which was originally such a disrupting influence on Anangu life, now provides different opportunities. The children are taken each year to Watson to sing to the passengers on the Indian Pacific train's Christmas in the Outback trip. In 2001 an extra carriage was added to take the children to Perth for a holiday provided by the railway company. The local band Desert Oaks also played for passengers on the special Tracks to Federation train in 2001. Now renamed Maralinga Desert Band, it sometimes plays at gigs far beyond. Working with visiting singer/songwriter whitefella Jeanette Wormald, children and adults have recently begun creating new songs celebrating their unique identity and life in Oak Valley. ●

Tommy Baker and Maxine Bridley, 2007 (Andrew Weller)

Ada Hart and Margaret May, Oak Valley, 2008 (Tom Stringer)

L–R Lyndon Williams, Lawrence Baker, Swayne Day, Yalata, 2008 (Tom Stringer)

Alinta Smart, Yalata, 2008 (Tom Stringer)

Kirsten Koko and Georgina Gibson, Yalata, 2008 (Tom Stringer)

Nathaniel Williams, Ooldea Soak, 2008 (Tom Stringer)

We Have Survived

Anangu have lived at Yalata now for more than half a century. Two generations have been born at Yalata and for these people Yalata is home. Gradually the lifestyle has changed from *wiltjas* to houses, movable camps to permanent settlement. But older people still like to sit around a campfire, and some still choose to live with their dogs in camps in the nearby bush. As well as houses, Yalata has a school, a health centre, a supermarket, a church, a women's centre and its own community council, football team, netball team, and newsletter, and some talented musicians. The community has produced its own CD of songs and music.

When Anangu first saw the coast beyond Yalata, the sea – 'big *kapi*' as Mr Minning described it – seemed strange, even threatening. But now people love to go to the beach for swimming, fishing and camping, as students Alinta Smart and Samantha Woods tell.

Alinta writes: 'I like to go fishing at Yalata Beach. We catch enormous mulloway in the sea. After we catch the mulloway we cook it in the ashes. It tastes good for all the family. I like to play in the waves and swim and look for shells.'

Samantha writes: 'I like to go fishing for salmon at Scott Beach and go hunting for malu, kangaroo. I like to go camping with Alinta. We dig for wombats and look for maku. I also like to catch sleepy lizard.'

After school, kids ride their bikes, go to the swimming pool, play netball at the Rage Cage, surf the net, or chill out with music at the Youth Centre. Some Friday nights there is a disco. At the 2008 Yalata Festival the school children acted, sang and danced in a performance of The History of Yalata to a full house.

Young people have to go to Adelaide to complete secondary school. Some go to the Lutheran Immanuel College. Some go to Woodville High School and stay at Wiltja Hostel for Aboriginal students.

Crystal Windlass and Nikisha Queama, Yalata, 2008 (Tom Stringer)

65

Two students, Sophia Gibson and Chari-Lee Peel, have successfully completed Year 12 studies and gained their South Australian Certificate of Education. Sophia now works in the Yalata clinic and Chari-Lee in the Koonibba child care centre.

Wiltja's motto is *Nguluringtja wiya.* (Don't be afraid.) *Ngulaku ngurkantara.* (Choose for the future.) *Pulkara nintiringama.* (Keep on learning in a big way.)

Some Wiltja students share their hopes and ambitions for life in ten years time:

Travis Dodd says: 'I would like to be living in Yalata. By then I will be 27. In the meantime I hope to be in training at SAPOL Police Academy at Largs Bay. To do that I need to finish SACE. I hope to get a job in Yalata community, living in my own house with my cousins and friends. On my days off I want to go hunting and fishing with my family and friends.'

Danielle Bridley says: 'For now I want to live in the Yalata community. I want to be a pool worker. I want to have a child, a little boy. At 26 I want to travel far away.'

Sasha Edwards says: 'I will be 23. I want to live in Yalata and work as a swimming instructor or a construction worker. I want to have a good life and a car and one big dog.'

Sally Williams says: 'In the future I could work in the clinic at Yalata Community, and live with my family. To be a health worker I will go to Adelaide for training, then learn some more in the clinic. In the holidays I could go somewhere special like the beach or out bush with my family.'

Ashley Stewart says: 'When I'm older I'd like to live at Oak Valley. I want to go to university to learn the things I need to know to be a teacher. I will need to keep on learning at school.'

Our people have had to adapt to many challenges and changes since they were removed from Ooldea over 50 years ago. Old and young have suffered many hurts and much unhappiness. Our land has been contaminated, sacred sites have been devastated. But we have survived. We are now two communities – Yalata and Oak Valley. But together we are still one people.

Deeply respected Mr Minning shares these wise words: 'Don't look back or take wrong ways. Look forward. Teach the children. Teach the young fellas. Look and listen and learn. Be happy.'

Maralinga – the Aṉangu Story is our story. We have told it for our children, our grandchildren and their children. We have told it for you. •

67

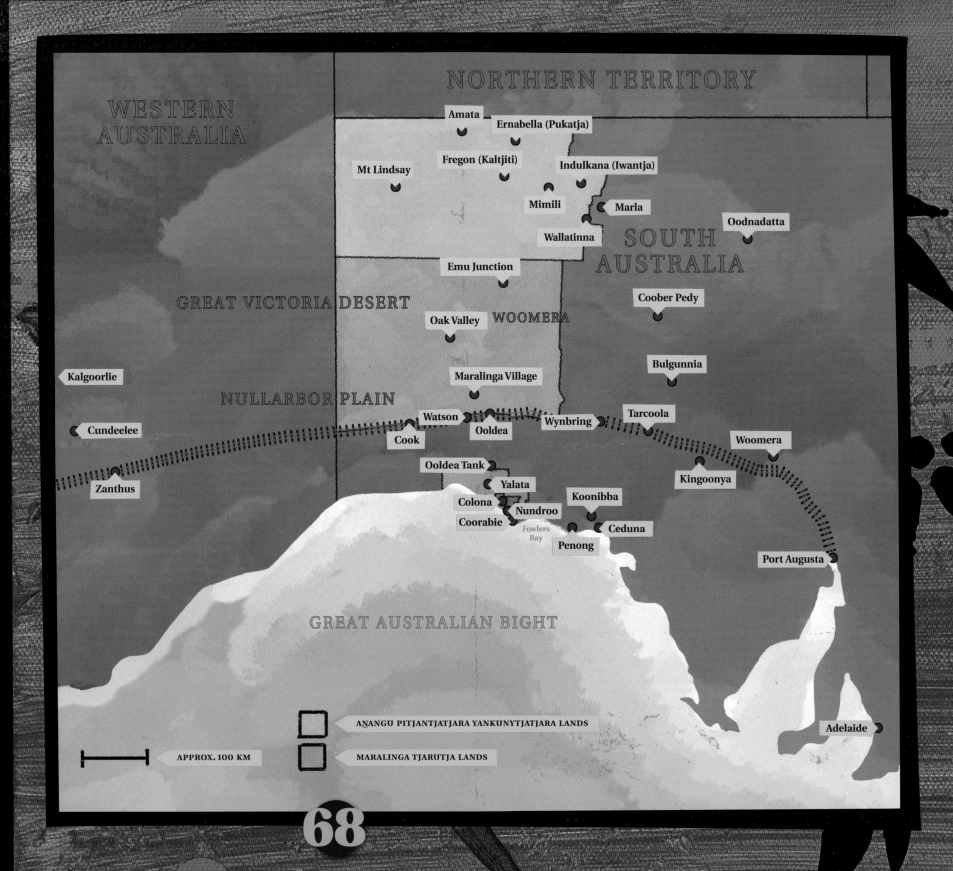

Glossary

Pitjanjatjara is the language most widely spoken by the Western Desert peoples.

Anangu	people; name used by peoples of the Western Desert when referring to themselves
ili	wild fig
inma	songs, ceremony, dances
kalaya	emu
kali	boomerang
kalta	sleepy lizard
kampurarpa	desert raisin
kapali	grandmother/granddaughter
kapi	water
kapi piti	soak
kipara	bustard, bush turkey
kuka	food
kungka	girl
maku	witchetty grub
malu	red kangaroo
mamu	evil spirit
mangata	quandong
mantara	clothes
mina ilu	thirsty
minyma	woman
miru	spear thrower
muruntu	snake
nganamara	mallee fowl
ngintaka	goanna
ngura	home, camp
nikiti	naked
nyapari	lerp, sweet insect casing found on gumleaves
nyitayira	boy
palya	good
pana	earth, land
pilangkita	blanket (from English)
piti	wooden dish
rapita	rabbit (from English)
tampa	damper (from English)
tjamu	grandfather, grandson
tjilpi	old man, grey-haired
tjintjira	claypan
tjinytjulu	gumnut
tjirilya	echidna
tjitji	child
tjiwa	flat grind-stone
tjukula	rockhole
tjukurpa	stories, the Dreaming
tjukurpa iritija	stories from long ago
tjunanpa	smoke
tjuta	many, lots, used to indicate plural
tuuni	thunder
walypala	white man (from English whitefella)
waltjapiti	family, gathering of relations
wanampi	water snake that guards waterholes
wangunu	a grass seed used to make flour
waru tjaa	firestick
wati	initiated man, man
watu	wombat
wayanu	quandong
wiltja	shelter
wira	wooden scoop or cup

Pronunciation: Curl your tongue back slightly to say the underlined consonants. 'Ng' at the beginning of words sounds like the end of sing.

Acknowledgements

Those involved in the planning of the book with Christobel Mattingley were:

Alice Cox, Yvonne Edwards, Janet May, Margaret May, Dora Queama, Mabel Queama, Marjorie Sandimar, Mima Smart, Pansy Woods. Mima Smart translated and interpreted for Alice Cox, Margaret May, Mabel Queama and Pansy Woods.

Art work by:

Audra Bridley, Noelene Bridley, Martina Boogar, Terence Edwards, Yvonne Edwards, Janet May, Josie McArthur, Hilda Moodoo, Dora Queama, Mabel Queama, Marjorie Sandimar and Mima Smart.

We would like to thank the following people and organisations for their help:

Ali Abdullah-Highfold, Diat Alferink, Dr Maggie Brady, Chris Brandwood, Peter Buckskin, Susannah Chambers, Andrew Collett, Maria Comino, Sandra Conte, Noelene Cox, John Dallwitz, Tanya Darke, Vivien Deed, Ashley Dorr, Bill Edwards, June Edwards, Max Fatchen, Tom Gara, Lea Gardam, Dr Heather Goodall, Chris Goulding, Chris Guille, Stevie Harrison, Graham Jenkin, Peter Kolomitsev, Lyall Kupke, Christine Langan, Bob Lines, Mabel Lochowiak, Michele Madigan, Canon Peter Patterson, David Rathman, Bob Sim, Craig Smith, Tom Stringer, Val Surch, Margaret Tischler, Erica Wagner, Philip Watkins, Cindy Watson, Andrew Weller, Nadia Wheatley, Jan and Geoff Willsmore, Andrew Wilson, Greg Wilson, Jeanette Wormald, JD Somerville Oral History Collection, Languages & Multicultural Resource Centre, Lutheran Archives, Nunyara Conference Centre, Oak Valley School, South Australian Museum, State Library of SA, State Records of SA, St David's Anglican Church Burnside, Tandanya National Aboriginal Cultural Institute, University of Adelaide, Barr Smith Library, University of SA Library and Yalata School.

We are grateful for financial assistance from:

Arts SA, Australia Council Community Cultural Development Program, Australia Council Aboriginal and Torres Strait Islander Arts Board and Maralinga Piling Trust.

Statements and information from:

Alice Cox, Yvonne Edwards, Margaret May, Mabel Queama, Mima Smart, Myra Watson and Pansy Woods are from interviews with Christobel Mattingley.

Other statements and information from:

Jack Baker, Freda Beara, Henry Beard, Danielle Bridley, Sandra Bridley, Veronica Bridley, Eileen Brown, Mervyn Day, Travis Dodd, Sasha Edwards, Girlie Ingomar, Kanginy, Kanytji, Kukika, Lallie Lennon, Yami Lester, Jack May, Judy Mayawarra, Edie Milpuddie, Stanley Minning, Hilda Moodoo, Gracie Peters, Kumana Peters, Kumana Queama, Tommy Queama, Rene Sandimar, Alinta Smart, Joe Smart, Ashley Stewart, Bobbie Stewart, Girlie Watson, Myra Watson, Sally Williams, Hughie Windlass, Pansy Woods, Samantha Woods, Heather York and Steven York.

Sources

SLSA = State Library of South Australia
NLA = National Library of Australia
SAMA = South Australian Museum Archives

Anangu interviews, evidence and transcripts from
the Royal Commission into British Nuclear Tests
in Australia, 1985

BOOKS AND REPORTS

Bates, Daisy. *The passing of the Aborigines.*
London, John Murray, 1938

Berndt, Ronald and Catherine. *From black to white in
South Australia.* Melbourne, Cheshire, 1951.

Bolam, A.G. *Trans Australian wonderland.*
Melbourne, McCubbin, James Press, 1923

Cane, Scott. *Something for the future: Community
Development at Oak Valley, S.A. Report to Oak Valley
Community and ATSIC,* 1992

Cross, Roger and Hudson, Avon. *Beyond belief:
the British bomb tests: Australia's veterans speak out.*
Adelaide, Wakefield Press, 2005

Davis, Peter S. and Brian K.Kirke. *Kapi Palya:
Meeting the water requirements of an Aboriginal
community at Oak Valley, Maralinga Lands, South
Australia.* Adelaide, SA Health Commission, 1991

Duguid, Dr Charles. *Doctor and the Aborigines.*
Adelaide, Rigby, 1972

Eames, G.M. and A.C. Collett. *Final submission by
counsel on behalf of aboriginal organizations
and individuals to the Royal Commission into
British Nuclear Tests in Australia,* 1985

Eyre, Edward John. *Journals of expeditions of discovery
into Central Australia and overland from Adelaide
to King George's Sound in the years 1840–1.
Volume 1.* Adelaide, Libraries Board of South
Australia Facsimile Edition No. 7, 1964

Goddard, Cliff (ed) *Pitjantjara/Yankunytjatjara to
English Dictionary.* Alice Springs, IAD Press, 1992

Hampel, N. A. *Yalata Lutheran Mission 1952–1977.*
Yalata Lutheran Mission, 1977

Lester, Yami. *Yami: the autobiography of Yami Lester.*
Alice Springs, IAD Press, 1993.

Mattingley, Christobel and Ken Hampton. *Survival in
Our Own Land: 'Aboriginal' experiences in 'South
Australia' since 1836.* Adelaide, Wakefield Press, 1988

McClelland, J.R. *The Report of the Royal commission
into British Nuclear Tests in Australia. 2 vols.*
Canberra, AGPS, 1985

Morton, Peter. *Fire across the desert: Woomera and the
Anglo-Australian Joint Project 1946–1980.*
Canberra, Dept of Defence, 1989

Palmer, Kingsley and Maggie Brady. *Diet and dust
in the desert: an Aboriginal community,
Maralinga lands, South Australia.*
Canberra, Aboriginal Studies Press, 1991.

Salter, Elizabeth. *Daisy Bates.* New York, Coward,
McCann & Geoghegan, 1972.

Turner, Violet. *Ooldea.* Melbourne. S. John Bacon, n.d.

ARTICLES

Berndt, Ronald and Catherine. 'A Preliminary Report
of Field Work in the Ooldea Region, Western South
Australia'. *Oceania* Vol XII to XV, 1942–45

Berndt, Ronald and Catherine. 'A Selection of Children's
Songs from Ooldea, Western South Australia'.
Mankind Vol 4 No 9, November 1952

Brady, Maggie. 'Leaving the Spinifex: the impact of
rations, missions, and the atomic tests on the
Southern Pitjantjarra'. Rec.S.Aust.Mus. 20. 1987

Brady, Maggie. 'The politics of space and mobility:
controlling the Ooldea/Yalata Aborigines,
1952–1982'. *Aboriginal History 1999.* Vol 23

Brady, Maggie and Kingsley Palmer. 'Dependency and
Assertiveness: Three Waves of Christianity among
Pitjantjatjara People at Ooldea and Yalata in Swain,
Tony and Rose, Deborah Bird (eds), Aboriginal
Australians and Christian Missions: Ethnographic
and historical Studies.' Adelaide, Australian
Association for the Study of Religions, 1988

Brockwell, Sally, Tom Gara, Sarah Colley and Scott Cane.
'The history and archaeology of Ooldea Soak and
mission'. *Australian Archaeolology,* 28, 1989

Goodall, Heather. '"The Whole Truth and Nothing
But …": Some intersections of Western Law,
Aboriginal History and Community Memory'.
Journal of Australian Studies. 35, 1992

Palmer, Kingsley. 'Dealing with the legacy of the past:
Aborigines and atomic testing in South Australia'.
Aboriginal History 14:2, 1990

Wallace, Noel. Pitjantjatjara decentralisation in north-
west South Australia: spiritual and psycho-social
motivation, in Berndt. R.M. (ed), *Aborigines and
change: Australia in the 70s.* Canberra, AIAS, 1977

White, Isobel. 'From camp to village: some problems
of adaptation', in Berndt, R.M. (ed), *Aborigines and
change: Australia in the 70s.* Canberra, Australian
Institute of Aboriginal Studies, 1977

White, Isobel. 'Mangkatina: woman of the desert',
in White, I.M, Barwick, D. and Meehan, B. (eds),
Fighters and Singers. Sydney, Allen and Unwin, 1985

VIDEO

Petrola wanti, Yalata Community, 1993

First published in 2009

Allen & Unwin
83 Alexander Street
Crows Nest NSW 2065
Australia
Phone (612) 8425 0100
Fax (612) 9906 2218
Email info@allenandunwin.com
Web www.allenandunwin.com

National Library of Australia
Cataloguing-in-Publication entry:
Maralinga : the Anangu story /
Yalata and Oak Valley Communities;
with Christobel Mattingley
9781741756210 (hbk.)
Aboriginal Australians – South Australia –
Maralinga. Anangu (Australian people)
Maralinga (S. Aust.) – History.
Mattingley, Christobel, 1931-
Oak Valley Aboriginal Community.
994.20049915

Research, text and compilation of material by
Christobel Mattingley
Jacket photos by Jan and Geoff Willsmore
and Tom Stringer
Cover and text design by Bruno Herfst
Printed in China by 1010 Printing International LTD

10 9 8 7 6 5 4 3 2

Teachers' notes available from
www.allenandunwin.com

This project has been assisted by the Australian
Government through the Australia Council, its arts
funding and advisory body.